Dogs As Family Members

How to Understand, Care For, and Train Your Family's Dog

by
James Akenhead, Ed.D.

Certified Professional Dog Trainer, CCPDT
Certified Dog Behavior Consultant, IAABC
Certified Professional Trainer, Nat'l K-9
Certified Dog Trainer, IACP

www.Signaturek9dogtraining.com

Visit our website and read client reviews to learn more about the effectiveness of our approach.

CCB Publishing
British Columbia, Canada

Dogs As Family Members:
How to Understand, Care For, and Train Your Family's Dog

Copyright ©2018 by James Akenhead
ISBN-13   978-1-77143-368-6
First Edition

Library and Archives Canada Cataloguing in Publication
Akenhead, James, 1943-, author
Dogs as family members : how to understand, care for, and train your family's dog / by James Akenhead. -- First edition.
Issued in print and electronic formats.
ISBN 978-1-77143-368-6 (soft cover).--ISBN 978-1-77143-369-3 (PDF)
Additional cataloguing data available from Library and Archives Canada

Front cover photo credit:
Fred Cockrill, Master Photographer, Cockrill Studio, Alliance, Ohio

Back cover photo credit: Shannon Harsh

Disclaimer: Please consider the Liability Waiver contained in Section 12 of this book to be in effect for you as a reader. If you cannot accept this waiver as presented herein, do not continue reading. Finally, never do anything with your dog that seems risky or dangerous, unless you have qualified firsthand personal advice from a professional trainer or behavior worker.

Extreme care has been taken by the author to ensure that all information presented in this book is accurate and up to date at the time of publishing. Neither the author nor the publisher can be held responsible for any errors or omissions. Additionally, neither is any liability assumed for damages resulting from the use of the information contained herein.

All rights reserved. No part of this publication may be reproduced, stored in a retrieval system or transmitted in any form or by any means, electronic, mechanical, photocopying, recording or otherwise without the express written permission of the publisher.

Publisher: CCB Publishing
             British Columbia, Canada
             www.ccbpublishing.com

Dedication

Rebecca Park, Certified Dog Professional
Among the very best. Left us too soon.
Missed by all of us.

Testimonials

The following comments are from professional dog trainers who were invited to read *Dogs As Family Members*; offer whatever suggestions occurred to them; and to offer a final comment for print here.

"I really enjoyed reading *Dogs As Family Members*. This book is a solid guide to growing healthy, loving relationships between a dog and his family members. This relationship-building process is simple--but not easy; it is a 24-hour endeavor. Jim not only tells you how to do it, but also tells you why you are doing it, which, I believe, is critical."
- *Sharon Blackstock, CPDT-KA and CGC Evaluator*

"Jim's style of writing is not only easy to read and comprehend, the concepts are easily implemented and utilized in everyday life, which can be quite intense and chaotic with rescue dogs. His down to earth style of communication is open and honest in its presentation of basic, easy to grasp concepts related to the relationship with our canine companions. Jim's extensive background with large working breeds was invaluable in supporting our team in the integration of several adolescent German Shepherds from various rescue backgrounds into our family environment over the years. He not only recognizes the need to acknowledge each individual dog and their personalities, but also the dynamic of the world view and personality of each of the handlers involved in the development of a comprehensive management plan."
- *Mary Ann Gasper, German Shepherd Rescue*

"Jim helped me to understand that dogs are not motivated out of stubbornness or retaliation. They simply do things that make sense to dogs. Once we understand that, we can *positively* communicate to them what behaviors we want or don't want in a language that makes sense to them and in an environment that fosters mutual trust and understanding. Jim's guidance in implementing a consistent training plan with *positive* reinforcement enabled Gracie (a very reactive German Shepherd) and me to cultivate the rewarding relationship that we share today."
- *Nancy Plavan, CPDT-KA, AKC Canine Good Citizen Evaluator*

"There is so much from this book that I use it took me a while to identify what I felt was especially important. Without this knowledge it would take so much longer for people to work with their dogs. That gem is learning to understand the difference between labels and behaviors when assessing a dog and what is occurring. As he says in his book, *Dogs As Family Members,* 'The first step is to move past mere labels ('Rover barks all the time') to specific accurate behavior descriptions that have clarified the situation more precisely (*'Rover barks for 10 minutes whenever I tie him to the tree behind the house in the afternoon'*). A mere label can't be quantified or specifically addressed, whereas a behavior description can be.' I keep this in mind with every client, and it has helped immensely in finding solutions that are workable in everyday life."
- *Diane M. Spencer, CPDT-KA & Therapy Dog Evaluator*

"Jim Akenhead knows dogs. Within the pages of *Dogs As Family Members* you will find 70 years of training wisdom that creates great pets."
- *Moira Bell, Editor*

The following are client reviews of my work using the model presented in *Dogs As Family Members*.

"Excellent! Your book *Dogs As Family Members* is the most informative and helpful that I have ever read. Wish I had known about it before I purchased some others."
- C. and B. W.

"We thought we would give you an update on Rufus. The holidays can be stressful for us humans as well as our pets. We did very well with company on multiple occasions and one evening I was almost concerned that he was behaving too well. I kept telling everyone that the real Rufus could emerge at any time. The only time he became less than what we hoped for was when he was provoked and that should not have happened. It proved to me that no matter what you tell someone or how many times you tell them, the responsibility is ours to make sure everyone is doing what they should be doing and are where they belong. Rufus also did very well with a dog sitter for a week recently."
- M. K.

"I've been meaning to let you know how well Toby is doing. He has come so far. He was such a mess when we first got him. I was pretty much resigned that he was 'as good as it gets.' Then we met you, and you believed in him. Toby is the most wonderful dog that I have ever known. And you have certainly helped him become the dog that he is today. I am so grateful for your help. You knew that he could improve, and you kept on helping him. He is a testament that dogs really are resilient and they can learn trust, respect, and love, even if they have never had these. We had had him for quite a while before you ever met him. He had already been expelled from dog school; all I ever wanted for Toby was for him to be a

regular dog. As you know, he was far from regular when you first met him. So I had to let you know how 'regular' my wonderful boy has become. I know that most of the credit goes to you, who tirelessly and patiently worked with him to desensitize him to other dogs. I just had to thank you again for all that you have done to help my boy. We were so fortunate to have found you."
- *N. U.*

"I cannot thank you enough for all you taught me at the puppy class. While I attended with my Sheltie, Arrow, you repeatedly emphasized the need to be able to get our dog's attention and to come when commanded. So, those were the two big things I have been working on with Arrow daily and it paid off big time. Thank you for your lessons, I still have Arrow and he is alive after a very traumatic incident. I take Arrow on walks with me daily, always on his lead, and a few days ago I decided to walk in another direction down our road. We live out in the country and I had walked about a mile and a half and decided to walk back home. We were about a mile from home when another dog came out of nowhere and was heading toward us. I urged Arrow to continue to walk with me, but that dog grabbed Arrow by the tail and ripped Arrow out of his collar and started to drag Arrow into the grass. Arrow was able to get out of the dog's grasp and began running away from me with the other dog close behind him. The dog got Arrow again and this time got Arrow's hind leg and I heard Arrow let out yelps of pain. Meanwhile I was yelling at the dog to get away. When Arrow finally got out of the dog's grasp, I commanded him to come and Arrow obeyed and came to me. I snatched up Arrow and walked away, and for reasons I don't know the dog did not pursue me. Once I was sure we were far enough away from the attack dog, I put Arrow down and placed his collar back

on him and checked him over for injuries. I knew he was in pain and he limped when he tried to walk since his hind leg was injured. The next morning my vet checked Arrow out and cleaned up his leg wound. The dog had bitten him and Arrow was badly bruised, but he will heal completely. I am just so thankful to still have my dog. Arrow and I have to give you some of the credit. If I had not attended those classes, I don't think this would have had such a happy ending. Thanks again!"
- J. W.

"Jim Akenhead, Ed.D. and his wife, Charlene, saved our overly dominant Dog Argentino's life. That is the easiest way to put it. Aja was born with a strong prey drive and was a tough customer growing up. With Jim Akenhead's help and great patience, Aja became a manageable pet and part of our family. At a time when we felt hopeless and thought we may have to put her to sleep for our safety and hers, Jim gave us the training we needed. With his help, she became a better behaved dog and we became better owners! We owe the happiness in our pet 'family' to him and Charlene."
- H. A.

"I am writing to let you know of the change that you have brought about with Venus, our German Shepherd. I took her to the vet today for her annual physical and shots. 1) An office employee walked up to her uninvited, extended her hand and gave Venus a treat. 2) Moments later another employee walked up to Venus and asked me to take Venus over to the scales. 3) I walked her into an enclosed examining room and waited for the vet. 4) He walked in with an assistant and slowly petted Venus and his assistant was at his side. (This room was no bigger than 8ft. by 10ft.) He proceeded to give Venus 2 shots, take a blood sample, do a glaucoma

screen, check her rectal glands, check her teeth, and cut her nails. All this was done without incident. Was she nervous, at first yes, but she seemed to relax. I did cheat a little. I took some liver treats along to give her occasionally. I wanted to tell you this to let you know the fruits of your labor. Thank You Very Much."
- B. F.

"It is exciting to see the progress that our Sheltie has made since going to Signature K-9. We adopted Finn in January 2008, after his first owner returned him to the breeder. We were told by the breeder that he was shy and liked to stay close to his human. I thought I knew what he needed… so to boost his self-confidence I enrolled him in classes at another facility. Little did I know!! What I thought was good for him only made his 'shyness' escalate into fear aggression. Then one day he bit my 2-year-old grandson. That was my wake-up call! We had become very attached to Finn by that time and we were not willing to just 'throw him away.' He is a sweet, funny and loving companion and worth a second chance. So I started searching for a professional and discovered Signature K-9. I e-mailed Jim and explained what we were dealing with. He reassured me that they had worked with this kind of problem before. Jim worked out a personal training program to help Finn while teaching me the tools I needed to be a more patient, relaxed and confident owner/handler. Finn has graduated from private lessons, to a 'reactive dog' group class, and now a puppy class where he is doing great and his self-confidence is growing. Each week I am amazed at what he has done. We are looking forward to the day that Finn is no longer afraid and we can take him for a walk in the park. Jim, Charlene, and Hollie show a genuine love and concern for each dog that comes through their door. Be it a shy, reactive Sheltie or an exuberant Golden Retriever, they are all

treated with patience and respect. Thanks Jim, Charlene, and Hollie!"
- C. A.

"I went to three other training facilities before finally finding Signature K-9. My Rottweiler puppy was not only unruly, but she had bitten me twice hard enough to draw blood when I had attempted to take a chicken bone from her. I was in way over my head and decided I needed professional help. Like I said, I went to a few other facilities first and I just wasn't satisfied with the level of expertise I received from them. The other trainers seemed confused and unsure when I explained my pup's behavioral issues. Even worse, the techniques they suggested were making her worse! Desperate to resolve my pup's issues, I kept looking. Upon discovering Jim and Charlene at Signature K-9, I quickly learned that not all trainers are created equal. They both had extensive knowledge of canine behavior and psychology and were quickly able to come up with a feasible plan to change my pup's behavior. Their methods were fun, humane, and highly effective. Not only did my relationship with my dog improve dramatically, but I gained so much confidence in myself as a handler that I was able to add another dog to my household. Now both of my dogs still attend more advanced classes at Signature K-9. One of my dogs has recently passed his CGC and therapy dog test. My other dog is being prepped for competition. They are both thriving and are a joy to have in my household. I could not have done this without the training and support I received at Signature K-9. I highly recommend them to anyone who loves their 4-legged friend!"
- H. T.

"My daughter and I took our German Shepherd pup to Signature K-9 Training and had a wonderful experience. Jim

was so calm and patient that his energy was contagious to both dog and owner. Through the class we learned so many valuable lessons that we still are using even after moving 1,500 miles away. Techniques such as the recall command, learning to stay in 'place' while we are eating and many other training tools has helped us immensely with having a well-behaved and enjoyable member of our family. I would highly recommend Signature K-9 Training for anyone who wants to have an incredible experience for both dog and owner. Thanks Jim and Charlene."
- *L. G. D., Colorado*

"My husband and I have two rescue Boxers; one male and one female. In regards to rescues, I was under the impression that if you just take the dogs to a safe home and give them enough time to realize it was safe, they would eventually come around and be fine. I was very wrong. We started reading books, got DVDs on dog behavior, took them to training classes, and exercised them every day, but it was not enough. Our male would still occasionally lash out at our female for what seemed like no reason. There was always a lot of tension in the house. Then the male bit me while I was trying to break up a fight. After the biting incident we realized how dangerous the situation was because there were children in the house at the time, so we called around for some advice. We were advised by experienced people that some dogs cannot overcome their past abuse and they suggested he be euthanized. I am very attached to my dogs, and I had to give them one more chance. I called my vet which led me to Jim.

 I was extremely hesitant at first because I have heard stories of 'trainers' and 'behaviorists' who do not use humane methods and I didn't want to get caught up with one of those. After just a couple conversations with Jim I started to feel more comfortable. He seemed to be just as picky about which customers he accepted as I was about who I allowed to work with my beloved pets. So I set up our first session and it has been worth every penny, every second and every ounce of effort. Jim was extremely positive from the very beginning which made all the difference after being bit. Since then all four of us have had great experiences. Some of which include reversing the damage of Opus' past abuse and neglect, building a better relationship of trust between us and the dogs, building a better structured routine in the home for the dogs and teaching us how to act in the appropriate way so the dogs don't misinterpret our actions and intentions. We even learned how to play with our dogs properly. Who knew that was important? – Jim!

We have seen the level of confidence improve in our male, which decreases his need for self-defense based aggression or fear aggression. This new level of confidence has also enabled him to relax more and enjoy more out of life (us too). From there we worked harder on building more trust between us. By the last session our once dog-aggressive pet was focusing on me while an unfamiliar dog was in the room. My dog – the same one that bit me just a few months before – was trusting me. Just before we left that night, both dogs were just a couple feet from each other, and lying down. It wasn't just obedience, he actually trusted me. He was okay to have his back toward the other dog and lay down even to the point of lying completely and voluntarily on his side. I'm sure it seems simple for most people, but it was an amazing experience for me. Anyone who knows dog language can understand what a vulnerable position that is for a dog. As I said, I feel very connected to my male dog, but that day that connection became a more clearly defined relationship with the foundation of very strong trust. My dog has come a long way, but I was surprised at what that lesson did for me. I went home with a greater sense of accomplishment, confidence and

pride. Maybe his methods work on humans too! Although it has been work, in a lot of ways the work has been fun and absolutely worth it. We really enjoyed our time with Jim and the things he taught us. Thanks a million times for helping us keep our companion."
- R. F. and J. F.

"If you are looking for an instructor who believes in the philosophy of positive reinforcement/reward, Jim is the one for you! No harsh tactics used here! Jim offers suggestions for solving your dog's problems in positive and gentle ways. Thus, learning is enjoyable for you and fun for your dog. How did I hear of Jim and why did I seek his help? Believe it or not, I was talking with a person who had interviewed three different trainers and felt that he was by far the superior one. So... armed with that information, Calli and I sought his advice. You see, my goal for my then 2-year-old Wheaton Terrier and myself was to become a certified therapy dog team. However, Calli displayed her exuberant personality with constant 'talking back' (barking) and continuous leash pulling when walking. Of course, neither behavior is acceptable for therapy dog work. I needed to get this little 'bundle of energy' under control. Through Jim's offering of various positive training techniques and through his constant encouragement, we overcame these particular problems and are now certified. I truly believe that without Jim's help we would not have accomplished our goal. In fact, we had so much fun that we continue going to class and learning more each time we meet with fellow classmates. Would I recommend Jim? You bet-ya! Is he one of the best around... absolutely! He is a real professional... no doubt about it!! One last thought. His facility is kept spotless and he always has training tools on hand to aid you. He throws his heart and

soul into his work… you cannot only see it but you can feel it. He will go that 'extra mile' to help you."
- C. T.

"My vet recommended that I get some professional training for my pup, Maizie, because she was what he referred to as a 'shy dog.' His concern was that she might become aggressive if provoked. Since I had never taken any of my previous dogs for training, I asked friends for advice on whom to take her to and received many recommendations for Jim Akenhead at Signature K-9. Jim starts each dog with one-on-one personal training which was very valuable for Maizie since she was so shy. Jim is very knowledgeable about dogs and he seems to be able to communicate with them without saying a word. During our first lessons he immediately taught me ways to read my dog properly so I am able to anticipate her behavior. He also taught me ways to help Maizie cope with her shyness, which we still practice today. Maizie and I have also attended group training at Signature K-9 which helped us both in many more ways. I was very impressed with the way Jim worked with all the dogs and got them to respond. I found the lessons to be interesting, relaxed and fun. Maizie has responded well to training and she has come a long way from her early puppy days. I now enjoy taking Maizie for walks because she is the first dog I have ever had that walks beside me, rather than pulling me along. I wish now that I would have taken all my dogs for training because the benefits are so great. If you keep up with the training that Jim teaches, you will have a pet that will be an enjoyable part of the family."
- J. L. C.

"We brought our miniature Labradoodle, Chloe, to Signature K-9 at around seven months of age. She was very high-strung and demanded a lot of attention. She had been through puppy

training elsewhere but we were having trouble with her jumping, pulling, and getting possessive with non-Chloe objects. Getting a shoe or sock away from her was risking a finger! Jim was very calm and firm but loving with Chloe. His presence alone seemed to affect her. He spent a lot more time than the allotted time with Chloe and me working on getting her to listen by praising positive behavior (along with reward) and discouraging the negative. My husband and I laughed that a lot of the time, the training was more for us than Chloe! The group classes were small enough that he was able to work individually with each dog, helping them and the owners get the required response in a group setting. We can't say enough praise about Signature K-9 and would highly recommend anyone to take their dog there. The facility is immaculate and Jim and Charlene are extremely knowledgeable. They have a true love for dogs and for what they do!"
- G. C.

"I'm not sure who enjoyed the class more – Chamois or me! I'm also not sure who learned more – the dog or the human. Thanks for a great class. It's good to learn techniques for civilizing one's pet that don't involve platoon sergeant yelling or jerking on choke collars. We'll definitely be back for more! The class was low-key, atmosphere-wise, which relaxed both dogs and their owners and yielded positive results in training. When Jim walked among the dogs, every head turned and every tail wagged. It was amazing. The dogs all loved him. We humans think he is pretty great too."
- B. G.

"We brought Winston to Jim after two different trainers. Winston had a lot of territorial issues. He was a rescue from the pound. Judging by his behavior, we believe he had been

abused. Jim worked wonders with him. On Winston's first visit, all he wanted to do was bite Jim. By our 4th session, Winston was on Jim's lap. Winston had private training until he was able to control his outbursts. We are now ready to begin group classes. Jim has worked miracles with him and I highly recommend him to everyone. We've seen a huge difference. Winston still has a way to go – but we are beyond thrilled with his program."
- I. M.

"On the advice of a dog trainer, I took my then one-year-old Newfoundland, Emma, to Signature K-9. Emma had been in attendance at two other obedience schools since she was ten weeks old; and we weren't making much progress with obedience. That changed when we enrolled at Signature K-9. Much to my surprise, I learned, for the first time, that I was a part of the problem. Jim and Charlene made sure that I understood what I was to do in executing a technique properly. In addition, if a technique just wasn't getting the desired results, Jim was able to modify or suggest a different approach. So here we are, a year and a half later, and Emma is now a registered therapy dog as well as a student in advanced obedience classes. My plan is to remain in classes into the future. Positive results, that is what Signature K-9 can provide you."
- H. W.

"Buddy, a Shepherd mix, was four years old when his aggressiveness became a real liability for me. He had bitten two people and neither the groomer nor the vet could get a muzzle on him. It broke my heart to ask the vet about putting Buddy down because I had rescued that cute little stray when he was 8 weeks old. The vet said I might try Signature K-9 before I made my final decision. I didn't have much hope

because Buddy had been expelled from puppy school when he was 5 months old, but I wanted to feel I had tried everything before I had Buddy put down. I met with Jim and Charlene 3 times for private lessons and have attended two 4-week group classes. I really enjoy Buddy now! I am amazed at how I could see improvements weekly. Buddy is well on his way to passing the therapy dog test. There is no doubt in my mind that Buddy would be dead today if not for Jim and Charlene at Signature K-9. I am so grateful for their expertise and patience."
- J. A. W.

"Boris and Natasha are our 4-½-year-old Boston Terriers. They'd been with us since they were 13 weeks old and they seemed very well-behaved. The only problem we had was that Natasha must've thought she was a beagle because once she got on the scent of a rabbit, nothing could stop her. We were afraid she would either run 'till she dropped or run into the street and get hit by a car.

In spite of that fear, I didn't know any trainers, and didn't want to take her to anyone who'd be mean to her. I couldn't stand the thought of losing her, so I talked to 3 other trainers before I talked to Jim at Signature K-9.

When I talked to Jim, he said he would rather have seen her at 3 months, but he would be willing to work with her. We set up four individual sessions; the first three would be Natasha by herself, and the fourth time we would take Boris with us so he could be evaluated. My husband and I decided that I would be the one to take her since they were to be my companions.

From the very first day, I had a great respect for Jim because while he was explaining to me how the training would work, he was also talking to Natasha and gaining her trust. Not one time did he do or say anything that would scare her. The entire time she was in training, he treated her as if she was a part of his family. He always treated her with respect – never raised his voice, and never lost his patience with her.

Jim always had 'homework' for us to practice before the next session. There was never a doubt in my mind that Natasha would pass with flying colors – even though a couple of times I was afraid I might flunk! Natasha was always a proud little girl, but with Jim's training she just seemed to blossom. Not only did Natasha excel, but when we took Boris with us on the fourth lesson, he could do everything Natasha had learned in class (perhaps a tribute to what his owners learned).

As for the theory that you can't teach an old dog new tricks – we also have a mixed breed dog that someone dropped off about eight years ago who now sits like a champ! We recommend Signature K-9 to anyone who wants their dog to be the best that it can be."
- S. D.

"After purchasing a new Miniature Schnauzer puppy for our children, the excitement quickly diminished as we realized how lost we felt. We had never had an indoor pet and the reality of having a new addition to the family had begun to set in. Dunkin didn't listen, or sleep, he had accidents in the house, and chewed on everything in sight. Obviously we were very frustrated and began searching for answers. Thankfully, we found Signature K-9. Jim took the time to sit with us and discuss his philosophies on training appropriate puppy behaviors and how to make the new addition to our family a welcomed one. We signed up for individual classes and quickly realized it wasn't just Dunkin who needed training, it was us who needed to be taught how to address appropriate and inappropriate behaviors and how to properly reinforce the behaviors we desired.

The changes in Dunkin's behavior were immediate, even after only one class session he was a different puppy. It was truly astonishing. Jim was able to give us the guidance we needed to elicit the appropriate behaviors we desired from our new puppy. We have now completed the individual classes with Jim, and Dunkin and I have signed up for group classes. We look forward to maintaining our relationship with Jim and Signature K-9 and continuing to cultivate a loving relationship with Dunkin. We are happy to say Dunkin is now the enjoyable addition to our family as Jim said he would be. We would highly recommend Jim and Signature K-9 if you have a new puppy and feel lost."

- C. D.

Contents

Section 1: Important Stuff 1
Who This Book Is For 1
Our Approach 2
Why I Am A Guy to Listen To? 3
How I Write 4
My Repeated Caution 5
Typical Client Concerns 6
Research, Intuition, and Experience 6
About Learning 7
This Isn't Magic 8

Section 2: Basic Understanding About Dogs 9
Sobering Statistics 9
Aren't There Just Good and Bad Dogs? 9
Canine Intelligence and Breed Characteristics 11
Developing A Relationship 13
Family Protection 14
Family Structure 15
Boundaries in the Home 15

Section 3: Basic Understanding About Humans 17
Why Discuss Human Behavior in a Dog Book? 17
Identifying Our Own Style 18
Four Main Styles 19
Balancing Our Style 20
How Style Affects Comfort Level 21
What Style Do Dogs Want? 22
That Invisible Belief System 23
Why This Matters 24

Section 4: Understanding Puppyhood 26
    Time with the Litter 26
    Stages of Development 27
    Meeting New People 28
    A Rule of Thumb 29

Section 5: Puppy Care and New Dog Basics 31
    Veterinarian Relationship 31
    Dog License 32
    Purchase or Adoption Contract 32
    Registration 33
    Identification 34
    Rides in Cars 35
    Get in Front of Nipping and Play-Biting 35
    Massage Protocol 37
    Grooming 39
    Introducing the Bath 40
    A Safe House 41
    The Crate 42

Section 6: Feeding, Schedule, and Housetraining .. 44
    Dog Food 44
    Rituals and Housetraining 46
    Sample Schedule 47
    Amount of Food and Water 49
    Age of Accomplishment 50
    The Older Dog 50

Section 7: Chewing, Toys, Exercise and Play 51
    Chewing 51
    Toys in General 53
    Getting the Most Out of Toys 55
    Exercise 56
    Regarding Dog Parks 58

 Treadmills 58
 Fetch 58
 Rough Play 59
 Playing Tug 60

Section 8: Multiple Dog Families 63
 Dogs vs. Wolves 63
 What About Siblings? 65

Section 9: Two Schools of Thought 67
 The Traditional Approach 67
 The Contemporary Approach 68
 The Extremes 69
 Dogs Form Preferences 71
 Your Choice 71
 My Bottom Line 72

Section 10: Options for Training 74
 When to Begin Training 75
 Puppy School 75
 Group Classes 75
 Private Lessons 76
 Training in Your Home 77
 In-Kennel Training 78
 Make Sure Your Trainer is a Good Fit 78
 Locating Trainers 79
 Building Your Home Training Team 81
 You May Have to Get Tough 82

Section 11: Collars and Leashes 84
 Leashes and Long Lines 84
 Harness 85
 Head Halter 85
 Flat Collar 86

    Limited Slip Collar 86
    Slip or "Choke" Collar 86
    Prong or "Good Dog" Collar 87
    Electronic Collars 87

Section 12: Groundwork: Basic Stuff 89
    Our Liability Waiver 89
    The Complexity of Liability 94
    A Caution 94
    Getting to Know Your Dog 95
    The Interview 96
    Protocol: A Structure for Doing Things 96

Section 13: The Thinking Behind Our Training 98
    Explanation of Approaches 98
    Positive Reinforcement 98
    Food Treats 99
    Punishment 100
    The Poker Chip Theory 102
    The Role of Fear 102
    Trauma History 103
    Overprotection 104

Section 14: Communicating with Dogs 105
    The Communication Gap 105
    Formal and Informal Life 106
    Good Manners and Simple Cues 106
    Choosing Cues 108
    Consistency 109
    What's In It for the Dog? 109

Section 15: Training 101 - Symbolic Feeding 111
    Leadership and Bonding 111
    The Step-by-Step Feeding Procedure 111

    Then Up the Ante 114
    Summary 116

Section 16: Fundamental Cues 117
    The Cue and the Action 117
    The Lure 117
    "Sit" Position 118
    Fading the Lure 119
    "Down" Position 119
    What About "Stay"? 122
    The Release Cue "Okay" 123
    "Wait" 124
    "Good Girl, Good Boy" 124
    Reinforcement 125
    Random Treating 126
    Your Part 127
    Generalizing the Cue to Work Anywhere 128
    Duration and Distraction 129
    Distance 131

Section 17: Safety, Responsibility and Liability 132
    Thinking Ahead and Planning 132
    Case Example: Welcoming Guests 133
    Case Example: Stealing Food 133
    Being Around Other Dogs 134
    Caution About Dogs off Leash 135

Section 18: Dogs on Leash 137
    Leash Signals 137
    Puppies on Leash 138
    Leash Walking 139
    Equipment 140
    Teaching the Leash Walk 141

Section 19: Neutral Behavior 144
    An Important Alternative 144
    Ignoring Behavior 144
    Case Example: The Jumper 145
    How It Works 146
    Case Example: All Dressed Up 149

Section 20: Attention and Recall 151
    Confirm Your Foundation 151
    Attention Work 153
    Recall 157
    Informal Recall 158
    Formal Recall 158

Section 21: Building Duration 163
    The Crossroads 163
    Awkwardness 164
    Duration in "Down" and "Sit" 166
    If You Want No Awkwardness 173

Section 22: Nonverbal Cues 175
    Hand and Body Signals as Cues 175
    Teaching Nonverbal Signals 176
    Is the Clicker Quicker? 178

Section 23: Establishing Home Base 179
    Home Base 179
    Define the Goal 179
    Steps to Home Base 180

Section 24: Time Out 182
Time Out 182

Section 25: More Complex Problems 187
Hyper Dogs 188
Mental Health Issues 189
Separation Anxiety 191
Aggression 193
Owner Fear 195

Section 26: Supplements and Medications 196
Definition of Supplements 196
DAP Collar 197
Rescue Remedy 197
Prescriptions 198
Side Effects 198
A Beneficial Mix 199

Section 27: Problem Solving Strategy 200
Behaviors vs. Labels 200
Prioritize 201
Brainstorm 201
Detailed Plan 202

Section 28: Intuition 204
Definition of Intuition 204
Clarifying the Problem 205
Where Intuition Takes Place 205
Enhancing Intuition 206
Don't Force It 207
What You May Experience 207

Section 29: Final Words 210
    Remember My Goal 210
    A Consistent Teaching Approach 210
    Nothing Takes Place in a Vacuum 210

About the Author 212

Preface

With proper training and relationship-building, dogs are capable of becoming great family members. We have had dogs that fit so well into our family that they are barely noticeable as outsiders to the human condition.

The dog that lives with us today knows our signals for almost everything. I tell people he speaks broken English. His signals are so deliberate they can't be ignored.

Much of the time our dog relaxes and snoozes in different spots in our home. When people visit, he has been taught to politely accept petting and then return to one of his spots.

With all this as context, he can change from a foggy sleep state into a fierce protector when he hears something that he identifies as odd or frightening. This doesn't happen often, but when it does it is amazing to see.

Helping build this kind of relationship is what this book is about. Our goal is not only to tell you what to do but to help you understand why you should do it.

Section 1:
Important Stuff

Who This Book Is For

This book has been carefully written for thoughtful people who want great relationships with their dogs. Dogs are not TV sets that can be managed with a remote control. *They are living beings,* and it takes investment on our part to cultivate a mutually pleasant relationship with them.

We gave my foundation book, Thoughtful Owners, Great Dogs, to everyone who brought their dog to our facility for training or behavior help. This version is written to be even more user friendly without losing the important training concepts of our model. It allows a reader to implement training on his own, or use the book as a support and reference when selecting or working with a trainer.

If you don't yet own a dog, this book will still benefit you as you prepare to get one. It will help you assess your lifestyle and circumstances, as well as your needs and expectations. Armed with this knowledge, you can research dog breeds and make your choice responsibly.

If you are a new puppy owner, great! This book will launch you well and help you avoid common pitfalls. If you own a dog who is exhibiting problem behaviors, know that there are creative ways to see great improvement.

As you read through what I encourage puppy owners to do,

you may recognize some missteps that you realize would be good to go back and address. From there, you can proceed into my systematic approach.

Our Approach

When a client comes to us with their dog, we do these things:

1. Get a feel for the pet, taking into consideration characteristics of the breed and the influences of the home. Knowing the nature of the home is critical in relationship building while training.

2. Clarify the goals of the client, with a realistic understanding of the dog's breed and the commitment needed to attain desired goals.

3. Explain and demonstrate with the client's dog how our training works, then teach them how to do needed training activities.

4. Offer support and feedback with continued demonstration as the plan is implemented.

We aren't just training *dogs*, we're also training *humans*. Humans need to understand and govern their own behavior in relationship to their dog if they are to become calm and effective trainers.

Our model is very specific, and it establishes a positive human-canine relationship right from the beginning – it is our designated end game and the crux of all we do. We're not advocating dominance or control, but rather bonding and responsiveness on the part of both the dog and the owner.

Why Am I A Guy to Listen to?

My own relationship with dogs dates back to my youth, seven decades ago, when the model of dog ownership did not generally include them being in the house. My grandparents' generation had seen dogs as outside pets with a job. On farms, they ate scraps, protected the family, hunted, and herded livestock. If they chased or killed chickens they might be shot. Mostly, dogs were utilitarian possessions, seldom beloved family members.

In my own formative years, dogs were not generally allowed in the house, but we had a neighborhood dog pack. Each kid had a dog, even if this was not officially sanctioned by their parents. We had a Chow Chow, a Fox Terrier, a Cocker Spaniel, a Retriever, and a Shepherd in our pack.

Everywhere the kids went, the dog pack went. We all contributed food, and the dogs scavenged for food on their own. Our parents just didn't want dogs in the house. As time passed, some of the pack were killed on the road, some disappeared, and at least one died of disease.

Good vet care was not considered important. Keeping dogs on a leash or in kennels was also not important. All I experienced and observed during those years, contributed to my own understanding of dogs. Only after making a contract to improve my high school grades, did my parents allow me to have a dog who officially "lived with my family" for many years.

My lifetime of relating to dogs, studying human behavior (including a counseling degree), and witnessing the extremes of thought about dog training, led my wife and me to open a premier dog training facility. For almost 25 years, we've helped hundreds of pet owners create very satisfying relationships with dogs of all breeds.

It is significant for you to know, that we became known as a "last resort" training option, even for pet owners who had no success using other trainers' techniques. **What we do works.** The numerous requests for a written version of our philosophy and approach, are what lead to the first edition of this book. Ten more years of experience and new research have resulted in this edition.

How I Write

My approach will be to write just as I would talk to you if you were a client at our training facility. What I will cover represents the issues and concerns that show up most often. No book can cover every possible contingency. If you have been a client, you will recognize this as an overview of what you have heard, along with some additional information that we may not have had time to discuss in your consultation.

"We" will be used some of the time when referring to what goes on. This is because, in most cases, no one does it alone. I have great support from my wife, Dr. Charlene Akenhead, as well as other consultants, trainers and veterinarians we call upon. In some cases, my explanations may seem too detailed. I do this because some of my readers have never seen our training and without details, they would be left to make up what goes on, potentially missing key elements. I apologize if

I fall short in my attempt to make things clear.

I have used an open page format (large print and lots of white space) so you can write in notes and questions. This book can be your reference guide as you solidify the training protocol I teach.

You should know that it was with trepidation that I wrote my first book and this book. That's because, it seems the only thing two dog trainers can agree on, is what a third one is doing wrong. You see, dog trainers and behavior consultants are in the constant throes of discussion (or argument) about what is good training and good science. Even those with advanced degrees have disagreements, sometimes including vehement confrontations that produce hard feelings. I am well aware that I hold to core beliefs about dog training that others do not.

As this book's title confirms – I am writing to help you have your dog be a ***family member*** – *along the lines of the proverbial "man's best friend."* My methods are anchored in positive reinforcement and logical consequences, rather than in dominance or punishment. I'll explain why as we go along – or see Sections 9 and 13, if you want more understanding about that from the outset.

My Repeated Caution

As you progress through this program, please pay close attention to your personal safety. **If anything suggested here seems dangerous or risky to you, do not do it!** If you try a suggestion and run into trouble, I strongly recommend that you get help from a trainer or a behavior professional.

If you, or any member of your household, are aware that you are already afraid of your animal, I advise you to get help from a trainer or behavior consultant immediately.

Typical Client Concerns

Calls we receive encompass a wide range of problems. In this book, we include information on the questions that we hear most often. If you find that the guidance given does not help to resolve your problems, you should contact a dog trainer, behavior consultant, or Veterinarian with an interest in behavior. Some situations require specific problem-solving strategies or a carefully built management plan. Suggestions about what to consider, if you need to find help, are offered in Section 10: Options for Training.

In the world of dog behavior and training, things are changing all the time. New information comes to the forefront as new research is done. If you question something here, or something you are told by a trainer, get a second opinion. There are many paths to solving a problem.

My best advice is that if your second opinion suggests a punitive approach, get a third opinion. Punishment is very tricky to manage; it should not be used indiscriminately, and I believe it should only be done under the supervision of a trained professional who understands operant and classical conditioning and only uses punishment as a last resort.

Research, Intuition, and Experience

As I mentioned, good research can show us the way in many

cases. But because of the expense involved in conducting research, it is often incomplete. Research structure when using animals as subjects is difficult to manage, and use of small samples makes results more difficult to generalize. In the absence of clear research results, experience and the intuition of knowledgeable trainers and behavior professionals are often what generates the best road map.

About Learning

As you go through this book, you will be introduced to some new ideas and skills for working with your dog. One factor that will contribute to your success is a willingness to **stick to it when it feels weird**.

If you ever learned to drive a stick shift car, you likely remember how confusing it seemed at first – You had three pedals, but only *two* feet… and two hands, which were supposed to *"stay on the steering wheel"* , but what about changing gears, and running wipers and the turn signals?!

At first, the skills I will teach you in these pages may seem as hard to grasp as that manual transmission. But don't be dissuaded. You learned to drive, and may even enjoy it – and the same will be true here. Awkwardness at first will eventually give way to a smooth ride. So relax. Feeling awkward at first is normal.

Much like when a seasoned athlete must learn new plays, you will still have some uncomfortable times like the small adjustment you must make when switching from a four-speed to a five-speed transmission. You experience a few minor grinds, but no big problem. In this context, it's good to consider that if no discomfort is ever felt, growth may not be taking place.

This Isn't Magic

All trainers were at one time where you may be right now. They weren't born with their current knowledge and skill. They had to work to get to where they are now. What trainers do is not "magic." To continue to be at the top of our game, we must keep learning just like you.

Please understand, that **to try and psychoanalyze a dog does little good**. The real task is to identify unwanted behaviors, and devise plans to change them. In this process we see that behavior is not linear. When working with difficult problems, unexpected breakthroughs can occur when you least expect them; other times, it seems like progress occurs at a crawl. During these times it is important for us to keep a positive attitude and not give up on our plan.

Section 2:
Basic Information About Dogs

Sobering Statistics

Some sad statistics suggest that only about one third of new puppies live their entire lives in their first home. The other two thirds are abandoned, left in shelters, or given to others in the hopes that the right home will cure their "problem." Many of those that are given away are eventually euthanized. This adds up to millions of dogs being killed every year.

We have seen many owners who felt they had the "perfect" dog in the past and are finding their new dog to be a challenge. Perhaps it's been a very long time since they had a puppy, and they've forgotten what it was like as a youngster, or maybe that other dog was just wired to be more laid back.

There is a small percentage of dogs who may be considered dangerous in the sense that no matter what is done, they will not fit easily into a family setting. This small percentage in no way matches the number of puppies and dogs who are abandoned or euthanized for behavior problems each year. With the advent of more "no kill" shelters and new training approaches, these statistics may be getting better.

Aren't There Just Good and Bad Dogs?

Some people question if all dogs need to be trained. They wonder why some dogs seem so naturally "good" and others are so "bad." If they come to believe theirs is just a bad dog, they are tempted to simply get rid of the dog who doesn't seamlessly fit into their family without issues. They may hope that their active puppy will just "grow out of her hyper behavior." They may worry that if they start training too early, they might break their dog's spirit.

In reality, dogs' personalities vary tremendously and are influenced by genetics and environment (Nature and Nurture). Likewise, everyone has their own definition of what constitutes a "good dog." Some people want a dog to bark whenever someone comes on their property, while others don't like it when a dog barks. Some want a dog who is playful while others want a quiet, easygoing dog that will sleep in the bed with them.

Many owners do not think about how the specific behaviors of a breed or mix will fit in with their family. Often, a family will end up with a pet because the dog was inherited, he was taken in as a favor, he was a gift, he was cute or beautiful, he was small or large, he doesn't shed, or he was like a dog they had as a kid. I'm not criticizing any of those rationales, only pointing out that diverse roads lead to dog ownership.

Many owners are simply unaware of how to guide their dog to be the pet they want them to be. **With training (of the owner and the dog), unwanted behaviors can be prevented or changed in the vast majority of dogs. That's why I do what I do and why I wrote this book.** Even the dog who starts out as a mismatch can be adjusted and become a beloved pet.

Canine Intelligence and Breed Characteristics

All of us, at one time or another, wonder how smart our dog really is. Like parents, we want a bright child... I mean "dog." And we want ours to be at the top of the class. Fact is, "intelligence of dogs" has been written about and debated extensively. The problem with answering the question, "How intelligent is my dog?" is that each dog breed was developed for a particular purpose. When performing that purpose, members of that breed generally can't be beat.

Take the Bloodhound; no other breed can track like the Bloodhound. Or the Malamute, no other animal can move as much weight over as much territory on as little food, in as deadly an environment, as the Alaskan Malamute or its cousin the Inuit Dog. Or how about the Border Collie, often thought of as one of the smartest... at least where herding is concerned. And the Terrier... no dog is as fierce in a faceoff in a confined space as a Terrier.

If you go looking for a German Shepherd Dog, you may be impressed with the idea that your pup's parents were imported from Germany. Later you may find that your pup came from working lines bred to be military or law enforcement dogs. Working line dogs may have been selectively bred to be very intense. This intensity may not make that pup easy to live with over time as a house pet.

If you are looking for a Labrador retriever, you may want to differentiate from lines bred for actual hunting versus those bred to be pets. Good breeders will tell you the truth about their dogs. Those whose primary goal is to sell puppies may not. You need to be an educated buyer.

Bottom line: intelligence is related to the circumstances the dog lives in, and the genetic package the dog was born with. A great herding dog may be a very difficult pet to own if she gets inadequate exertion, and no opportunity to exercise her mind. When people ask about the intelligence of their dog, they are usually thinking in terms of compatibility in a home situation. In reality, not all dogs rank high on these criteria. In fact, a dog rated to have low intelligence based on ideas of traditional obedience, may be the smartest in her breed's specialty area.

As a family pet, some breeds fit well if a person has done research...not just looked at pictures. When a dog is obtained based on a realistic understanding of the circumstances the dog will live in, the result is usually satisfactory. Results can be good to excellent, if the human develops a clear structure and communication system with his companion.

Even a great dog is at a disadvantage when put into unrealistic circumstances. A common example is the large breed dog, perhaps a Labrador (known as a good-tempered breed) that is purchased as a puppy for an older parent or grandparent as a companion. As the dog matures and reaches adolescence, the situation can become untenable. The dog becomes so physically strong and active that, through no intent of his own, he makes life for his owner miserable. In some cases, the dog in this situation may be considered unintelligent because of his circumstances.

Finally, no matter what the breed, **an individual dog can make a liar out of any generalization**. A Malamute can make a great pet... but he is always a Malamute, and he will always have Malamute traits. Malamutes are very bright dogs and yet they are not always considered the easiest dog to train as a pet. This does not make the Malamute a low intelligence dog. Good training can help manage those traits. In cases where a dog has not been chosen to specifically match the family circumstances, a lot can be accomplished with a structure, good training and clear communication.

Developing A Relationship

To develop a great relationship, we must be aware of how we interact with our dogs 24 hours a day, not just when we want to give the dog a command to sit, lie down or behave. We need to be aware of the signals we send—both formal cues or commands (which we might use about 20% of the time), and in the ways we interact with our dogs informally (the other 80% of the time).

When you look at those numbers, you realize dogs are only on formal cue or command a small percentage of the time they spend with us. The rest of the time, they are expected to show the kind of manners that make our time together enjoyable. The problem here is that some people think dogs should automatically figure out what they ought to do to make us happy.

For the occasional wonder dog, this works. If you have owned one of these wonder dogs, it can make it all the more difficult to understand why it doesn't happen for all dogs. The fact is, if we don't make it a point to be clear with our dogs about all aspects of their life, they often get mixed messages about when it is okay to play, how rough to play, when to be a guard dog and when to relax and let our friends in the yard.

As human companions, we always need to be mindful of the

fact that until we teach the dog what we want him to do (our version of good manners), the dog is doing things that make sense to him as a dog.

Family Protection

Protection of the family is a hot topic. Many people, especially those with big dogs, hope that their dogs will protect them when the chips are down. Once they become attached to their family, many dogs are protective. That does not mean the dog understands what to do or when to do it. Having a dog that is trained to protect requires intense work for both the dog and the handler. Not all dogs are up to the challenge and not all handlers are willing to commit the time needed to do the basic training and the continued workouts that are necessary to keep the dog sharp. Even if all the protection training is done, one can never be sure if the family dog will perform under pressure.

A sharp protection dog knows what to do when *cued*. A clean dog *stops* when told. A protection dog who is not sharp and clean is dangerous. He may not protect when needed, and if he is not clean, he may bite when not appropriate or not let go when cued. In any of these cases, the dog may be put to death and the owner may be sued.

For most people, the presence of a family dog who is well trained in obedience may make the most sense. Such a dog is a deterrent just by being there. Certain breeds, such as the German Shepherd, seem more naturally protective, are a bit suspicious, and may be likely to ward off most unwanted intruders.

Family Structure

For harmony to exist, a dog must understand his place in the family hierarchy. This means that even though we may love the dog, we cannot treat him as a human. This does not make the dog less in our eyes. It just speaks to the reality that dogs are different and for things to go well, we've got to recognize those differences and create the correct structure in our family.

This requires confidence and consistent adherence to a plan that follows specific protocols when giving food, water, affection and attention. It also includes using symbolic activities that may help establish leadership and bonding.

Boundaries in the Home

Some people believe that dogs can develop an attitude—even become aggressive—if they are allowed to get on beds, chairs, couches and other furniture whenever they want. Others will tell you that there is no research to prove this. In fact, some mention informal surveys where large groups of respondents have indicated that they have dogs on beds and furniture with no problem.

In my experience, it is wise to consider that if dogs are given free rein with furniture and beds, it may lead the dog to perceive that he owns the territory thus claimed. As an example, when a dog is on a bed and a young child attempts to move the dog off, perhaps by pulling the dog's collar, if the dog assumes that he is entitled to be up on the bed, he may also feel justified in disciplining the child for invading his space. Although this may not occur in all instances, the risk is worth considering.

Further, we are aware of other instances where, once a dog settles in with the perception of higher status and then connects that with resource guarding, he may refuse to move from his favorite chair or bed even when requested by an adult. A case comes to mind where a male Mastiff would not allow the husband to share the bed with his wife. The only safe way for them to deal with the dog was to throw meat into the hall and quickly close the door locking the dog out.

After a dog has been with a family for some time and his behavior is clearly predictable, it may be safer for you to consider allowing the dog up on the furniture. My suggestion to clients is to make a conscious decision about this. Don't just let it happen.

If the decision is to allow the dog to get on beds, chairs or couches on his own, pay close attention to any questionable behavior that develops. My personal preference is to either keep my dogs down or have them come up on cue or at my request. This means using a cue such as "Up," accompanied by a pat on the lap or cushion. When the dog gets up, you acknowledge with "Good Boy." When you are ready for the dog to get down, say "Okay" and move the dog off. With this method, if the dog gets on any furniture any time when he has not been invited, tell him "Off" and remove him. You'll learn more about giving clear cues in Section 16: Fundamental Cues.

Section 3:
Basic Understanding About Humans

Why Discuss Human Behavior in a Dog Book?

It may seem odd to include a section about humans in a book about working with dogs. But when you think about it, humans are always at least 50% of the problem or 50% of the solution in any canine-human relationship. For that reason, leaving out consideration of what drives humans would leave a big hole in the puzzle we are putting together.

It's tricky to break down the components that drive humans. To do this in a practical manner, I've chosen a two-fold approach.

The first element, our style, can be seen through observable behavior. The second element is what goes on inside our heads as judgments are made about everything in life. While style can be readily observed, the belief system that is used to make judgments is more elusive.

When working with dogs or people, things always go better if we first know ourselves. We need to understand what kind of behavior we use most frequently, and what kind of impact our behavior has in various situations.

For a trainer or behavior consultant, it also means knowing enough about how styles work that we can identify the basic style of others. Understanding both self and others enables us to make conscious choices as we interact.

That second element, of our invisible (but very real) thinking system, isn't known unless it is shared or identified as we make decisions. It is the part of us that forms the belief system, that acts as a filter through which we view the world. This filter sets the "appropriateness" standard as we evaluate everything we see, hear, feel and do.

It is the combination of our style and our belief system that determines how we operate with others and with our companion animals. It is this combination of factors, and how we manage them, that determines our effectiveness in all relationships.

Identifying Our Own Style

It is of utmost importance that we know something about how we come across, and why we react the way we do, particularly under pressure and unconsciously. This gives us insight into why things sometimes go well (and sometimes not so well) when we are working with our dogs.

The first piece of the "style" puzzle is **personal awareness**. Are we a high-key Demanding Don, a light-hearted Social Sally, a laid-back Steady Eddy or a carefully controlled Analytical Alice?

We may all possess a little of each of these tendencies, yet it's common to prefer one or perhaps two of these styles over the others. This is not a conscious preference. Rather, it's something that we do naturally and without thinking.

Each of these general style preferences has inherent comfortable and uncomfortable ways of operating. Once we understand what our natural and most comfortable operating approach is all about, it's important to step back and look at how our approach works as we interact with our dogs and with others.

Four Main Styles

Here are the four predominant operating styles in the model I use:

In Charge (Demanding Don)

Those with a take-charge style do not like leaving anything to chance. They may also have feelings of conflict about others who like to be in charge. Those with this style are outgoing go-getters. They jump right in, take chances and assess the results later. They may be among the first to become up-tight with their dog if she appears to be defiant or not willing to do what she is told.

Social (Social Sally)

A person with a social-oriented style is outgoing and wants to have a good time. For this person, having fun is a criterion for success. If a situation seems tense or the dog seems to be unhappy, those with this style are likely to be uncomfortable and dissatisfied. If the relationship is not attended to, they may become discouraged and not want to go on.

Steady (Steady Eddy)

Those with a steady style are laid-back and level-headed.

They want everyone to get along. They don't like situations where conflict is present and will try to negotiate consensus. Those with a steady style may be concerned about pushing their dogs too hard. The relationship with their dog will be paramount. A sense of team is the preferred atmosphere.

Analytical (Analytical Alice)

Analytical people like details. They want to know the research and understand where opinions come from. They want to know why things happen. What makes the dog do this or that? Why won't the dog cooperate? Sometimes, psychoanalysis of the dog seems more important than solving the presenting problem. Not knowing the answers can cause this person much frustration.

These descriptions may help you get a handle on your own style. This awareness can help you be on guard and modify your style inclination to better relate to your dog as well as accomplish your goals.

For instance, if you know you get frustrated when you're not in control, you can intentionally work to remain relaxed and take a break if things get too tense. If you are more social or steady, you can convince yourself to hang in a little longer when you might otherwise want to quit. If you are analytical, you might allow yourself to trust a trainer with a good reputation to know what to do without giving you the minute details every moment.

Balancing Our Style

I am not suggesting that there is a best style. Instead, we need to recognize the strengths in our style as well as where a given style might make us vulnerable in some situations. This understanding enables us to consciously manage and enhance our potential for success.

In stressful situations there must be a balance between accomplishing a task and not ruining relationships. If you have a hard-driving personality style, your tendency may be to push your dog harder when things are not going well. If you have a steady, easygoing style, you may tend to back off every time things get the slightest bit confusing or frustrating for you or for your dog.

If you favor a more social style, you may be so interested in having fun that you can't go on if any stress exists. If you are more analytical, you may have so many questions about "why" that you never get to working on the behavior at hand.

A more desirable outcome is possible when we are committed to accomplishing the task while also being aware of the part our unconscious operating style plays in the process. It is this awareness that can make the difference.

How Style Affects Comfort Level

Style also affects success when it is related to our sense of comfort, particularly in new situations. We often feel uncomfortable in new situations or when we are learning something new. It's then that we may begin to doubt our competence. If we equate discomfort with the idea that we may not be competent, we limit our success.

If our most comfortable operating style tends to be structure and detail-oriented, we will probably feel most at ease in situations where we are operating in a highly organized setting with clear, step-by-step directions. Not only might we want a detailed explanation, we might want to see pictures of each step and then a live demonstration. We may not care about humor or charisma, and we might hate it if someone takes what appears to be a very loosely structured approach. Conversely someone with a very social style might wilt under matter-of-fact lists and details, without a strong sense of relationship with the trainer and social lightheartedness mixed in.

Along with awareness that style is strongly connected to our comfort zone, it is also important to realize that we are capable of adapting our style to fulfill most tasks and relationship needs. We only need to modify our style, based on the situation, to enhance success. And, when doing so, remember **that discomfort has nothing to do with our competence.**

To maximize our style, we must become aware of the circumstances that make us uncomfortable. We must understand that each person's style brings with it some natural strength and some vulnerability. Strength can then be maximized and we can offset vulnerability by conscious personal choice.

What Style Do Dogs Want?

According to one of today's top behaviorists, your dog may very well prefer you to have a personality style like Gandhi. My interpretation of that style is:

- Someone who can maintain their composure no matter what; a person who doesn't show frustration or anger to the dog.

- A person who knows when to get excited, when to remain calm and when to take a break.

- Someone who is clear and consistent about structure and guidelines.

- A person who can manage her style rather than let it manage her.

That Invisible Belief System

Unlike a basic human style that we are born with, we each have a personal belief system that developed over our lifetimes. The core beliefs upheld in our family, our religious exposure, and life experiences (the hurts and delights) all program us inside to "believe" certain things are true.

This lifetime of experiences is stored within our memory mechanism. And it is what directs the little voice deep inside us as we decide the way things should be.

Sometimes, that little voice is whispering so softly that we don't even realize it's present. Other times, such as when we back our car into a light pole, it screams at us with its opinions about how dumb we are, or what a stupid place that was to put a light pole.

Many of us are so unaware of this little voice that when the idea is first introduced, we deny its existence. With further examination, we may find that it is this very same little voice telling us that no such voice exists.

The question is, "Are we willing to consider that there is some mechanism, sometimes subtle and sometimes screaming, that drives us to judge what is right or wrong?" If so, then it is important to consider the origin and validity of information being used by that inner voice as it functions as judge and jury in our life.

As we mature, and interface with others of different beliefs, we modify and adjust what we believe to keep pace with new information. For example, in the past, the message was that there were a limited number of professions appropriate for women. Today we know that women can flourish in all fields of study. Someone who failed to see this shift and keep pace with it, still touting something like "A women's only place is in the home," would find himself woefully isolated and unable to relate to reality.

Why This Matters

I mention this to say, just as we need to take an honest look at our "style," we need to take a little inventory of our *beliefs* and expose them to some scrutiny. This has bearing in regard to dog training, because we all have beliefs about what constitutes a good dog, or a good relationship with a dog, and without clarifying and voicing these, we will have trouble finding a good training model.

We all must guard against the temptation to think that our beliefs came from irrefutable sources, or that we have superior viewpoints (or intelligence) that trump everyone else's.

For this reason, in my work, you'll see frequent use of statements such as "our current belief is" and "research seems to suggest" and even "my hunch or personal belief is." I will also be as forthcoming as possible with my core beliefs.

The short list of these include:

- I believe there is a force greater than I.

- I believe I am not capable of fully understanding this force or how it works.

- I suspect this force is involved in relationships between humans and dogs.

- I believe that life is precious and dignity is due to all life.

- I agree with the premise Do No Harm.

- I believe the definition of "harm" is tied to one's belief structure.

Section 4:
Understanding Puppyhood

Time with the Litter

Generally speaking, puppies should not leave their litter until they are at least seven weeks old. Some people believe that puppies can leave the litter as soon as they are weaned from their mother. This is not good practice. More than once, I have suggested that a potential client return a four or five-week-old puppy to his litter until he is seven weeks old.

Puppies learn from their mother and from littermates. Puppies removed early may miss valuable developmental lessons and social skills such as how to send and receive signals, how far to go in play, and understanding ranking – "who's in charge." Among littermates, they find out about "inhibited bites" (acceptable mouthing pressure). Skills not acquired during this time can result in behavior issues later. Although these problems may be able to be dealt with, they can cause frustration that is easily prevented, just by keeping the puppy with his litter for the appropriate amount of time.

Once you take the puppy home, he should be sheltered for about two weeks for observation. During this period, if the puppy becomes ill, it may mean that the illness started at the breeder's facility. If the puppy remains healthy during this period, you may be fairly sure that nothing has come home with him from the breeder.

Between eight and ten weeks of age, while the immune system matures, puppies should be introduced to as many people as possible in the safety of their home. During this time, it may be a health risk to take puppies to public places, including pet supply stores, where they might contact other animals who are transporting disease or parasites.

Stages of Development

Based on structured observation in controlled settings (done by Drs. John Paul Scott and John L. Fuller and published in 1965 in *Genetics and the Social Behavior of Dogs*), dogs are thought to develop in identifiable stages. Listed below is a view of these stages which I believe is accurate.

- **Neonatal Period (0–2 weeks):** Puppies are most influenced by their mother.

- **Transitional Period (2–4 weeks):** Puppies are influenced by their mother and littermates. Eyes open, teeth begin to emerge, the senses of hearing and smell develop. Pups stand, walk, wag their tail and bark.

- **Socialization Period (3–12 weeks):** From three to seven weeks, puppies need chances to interact with other puppies and people in the safety of their litter while housed in a clean facility. At seven weeks or older, when puppies come to live in their new home with humans, they need additional opportunities to meet other dogs and people. This is the time to ramp up opportunities for safe interaction.

- **New Home Socialization 7–12 weeks:** Puppies typically go to their new homes and begin a new phase of socialization. The key is to introduce them to experiences and people that are unlike those they encounter every day in their new home. Anything that is different from their home life will be of concern if pups don't learn early that different does not mean scary or untrustworthy. According to Ian Dunbar, if you could introduce your puppy to 100 people by the time he is 12 weeks old, it would not be too many.

The same idea is true for places. Take him places that are different from his home, such as a car wash, an elevator, strip malls, parks, anywhere he will experience different surfaces, sounds and feelings. Make it a point to think, "Where can I take my pup that he hasn't been?"

If these socialization activities are not done, reconditioning, if possible, can require a huge commitment and can take a long time.

Meeting New People

When your puppy meets new people, it must happen in a non-intimidating, non-threatening manner—from the dog's point of view. Remember, dogs and humans are different species. What we might think of as entirely harmless could have a different meaning in a dog's view.

Generally, I like to associate a dog-human meeting with a high-value food treat. This sets up a positive association. The puppy associates the treat with meeting new people... that's a good thing. If this is done regularly, over time it teaches the pup to look forward to meeting new people.

To ensure the new person does not appear to be intimidating or challenging to the dog, coach him not to look directly into the dog's eyes. Also, have the person turn slightly sideways, offering the treat in a flat hand at their side which is toward the dog.

If the puppy is hesitant to come up and get the treat, use the breadcrumb approach. Have the new person toss tiny bits of treat out to where the dog is, and gradually lure the dog in by tossing the treats closer. Don't reach out to the dog. Be patient. Keep this up until the dog is comfortable.

Do not let the new friend go to the dog. Let the dog move to the person. Keep new friends from leaning over the dog or reaching their fist out toward the dog. If your dog is nervous, it is very important that she does not feel forced to meet people. Take your time and use that breadcrumb approach. Trying to rush things may only make things worse.

Once the dog will take a treat from an open hand at the person's side on several occasions, move on to petting the dog, starting under the chin and neck, then along the side. If the dog backs up when petting is attempted, back off. Offer more treats until the dog is more comfortable. Be patient.

Once the dog accepts petting under the chin, you can consider petting the head. Over-the-head petting is easier for the dog once he knows and trusts a person. If your pup does not respond to this approach, you may need help from a trainer.

A Rule of Thumb

A rule of thumb is that anything you want your dog to do

as an adult is easier if it's introduced as a puppy. This can be seen in the so-called Superdog programs designed by breeders of dogs who work in the military, law enforcement, search and rescue and other high-demand occupations. In these programs, puppies are challenged by many experiences that are specifically designed so that a strong foundation of confidence is built.

Section 5:
Puppy Care and New Dog Basics

Here is a list of issues that must be addressed early on, or they can cause problems later. Even if your dog is older, there is valuable early ownership information here for anyone with a dog at home.

Veterinarian Relationship

Take your dog to the veterinarian within 48 hours after he arrives at your home.

- At that initial exam, discuss inoculation schedules, spay/neuter procedures, prevention of fleas and other external pests, prevention of heartworm and other internal worms, and exposure to dangerous diseases.

- Make a list of any questions you have and be sure to ask your veterinarian. Your veterinarian should be your first line of defense if a health problem arises.

- When a problem arises at home, most veterinarians are glad to answer some questions over the phone to determine if it is necessary to take your dog into the veterinarian's office.

- Your dog should have a yearly veterinarian appointment for a check-up. **Remember, every year in a dog's life is roughly equivalent to seven years in a human's life,** so that yearly veterinarian appointment is actually like checking a human every seven years.

Some diseases can advance rapidly in a period equivalent to seven years. Your dog's annual check-up can help keep you ahead of some tough problems.

- When an emergency occurs, that is not the time to wonder what to do. Identify the nearest veterinarian who offers emergency services, including night and weekend availability. Have those phone numbers available along with driving directions where everyone in the household or any pet sitters can quickly access them.

- Having a regular veterinarian for support and an emergency veterinarian when needed can make the difference between life and death for your dog. Best of all is when your regular veterinarian and your emergency veterinarian work together.

Dog License

Don't forget to check on when your pup must be licensed in your state or municipality. If your dog wears his tag on his collar, there is a better chance he will find his way home if he gets lost.

Purchase or Adoption Contract

Don't assume anything. Read the purchase or adoption contract and make sure you understand all of its provisions. For example, if your purchase contract says your pup will be replaced if he is diagnosed with severe hip dysplasia, via

X-ray, *on his second birthday*, that is different than wording that says *up to* his second birthday.

Keep receipts and any documentation necessary to verify that you have done the things you agreed to do. If you have a problem, the contract could be all you have to fall back on.

Registration

If applicable, remember to send in your American Kennel Club (AKC), United Kennel Club (UKC) or other registration papers.

- There are a variety of registration organizations for all kinds of specialty animals.

- Some breeds have their own registration systems and their dogs are not registered with the more common national associations.

- Some of these smaller registries exist because of the desire to keep tighter control over breed standards or because a national organization does not yet recognize a breed for registration.

- Mixed-breeds can also be given a special registration designation so they can compete in trials and competitions with the big national organizations. Each organization has its own requirements.

Identification

To increase the chances of recovering your dog if he gets lost, we recommend that you consider having your dog tattooed or microchipped. Check with your veterinarian about options.

- If you choose a microchip and your dog becomes lost, most shelters and veterinarians will check to see if he is chipped. Keep those ID numbers and registry phone numbers where you can easily access them, such as in your cell phone and home address book.

- If you opt for a collar tag, consider putting *family pet, reward and a phone number* on the tag. I was once told not to use the dog's name because it can help a would-be kidnapper make friends with the dog.

- On our tags, we put: *family pet, microchip, reward and two phone numbers,* ours and the one for the microchip company.

- Be sure you have a current photograph of your dog and a good written description. Creating a template for a Lost Dog poster on your computer, that you can add information to, will be helpful should you ever have to hand out flyers that your dog is missing. This will save you valuable time. Having a photo of you with the dog will also be a good way to help prove ownership, if necessary.

Rides in Cars

Some dogs love riding in the car and some become carsick. If you want your dog to be comfortable in the car, here's a good way to get started.

- Start with frequent, short rides the length of your driveway.

- Then drive around the block; then a little farther.

- Gradually increase the length of rides.

- Make the destination as positive as possible. So, for example, don't take the dog in the car only when it is time to go to the vet.

- Try feeding your dog in the car (while it's parked).

- Hide treats in the car so your dog regards it as a good place to be.

- If your dog continues to become ill when on rides, check with your veterinarian for medication options.

Get in Front of Nipping and Play-Biting

Keep your fingers away from the dog's face and mouth. If new owners would do just this with puppies and young dogs, they would eliminate a big part of this problem.

Puppies and young dogs play using their teeth. They use their mouths in much the same way, and for many of the same functions, for which we use our hands. Our job is to structure the play so they learn to keep teeth off skin and avoid nibbling on humans in ways that hurt.

Puppies learn some of this play structure from their littermates. They learn that when they bite too hard, they get a "yipe" response from their brothers and sisters. They learn that if they challenge mother, heaven forbid, there can be dire consequences. That's why it's important to keep puppies with their littermates for at least those seven weeks, even though they may be weaned.

Once the puppy joins our human family, we pick up the responsibility for teaching him. You can continue the "yipe" method when a puppy bites. That means the human must "yipe" like it hurts, even when it doesn't, and then ignore the puppy for several minutes. Ignoring should be done as described in Section 19. Generally, it includes closing up your body, avoiding eye contact, keeping your appendages out of reach, and not moving.

One key here is not to provoke behavior that results in nipping or biting. When it happens, ignore it. Wear appropriate clothes when you are training your puppy to play nicely, so that, while you are ignoring, the pup can't bite you. That means long pants and long-sleeve shirts—heavy clothing, if necessary.

Remember, **keep your fingers away from the front of the dog's face and his mouth**. If the dog bites, even a little nibble, stop interacting with him and either ignore him or move away from the dog. If he follows and nips, let him drag an attached house leash so you can control him. Try redirecting him to a chew toy or get him to play fetch. If these things don't work, put him in his crate or tether him until he settles down.

Playing by pushing the dog back and encouraging him to come forward and use his teeth cannot be a part of the play methods employed. You are encouraging play biting and mouthing and the results can be calamitous, especially as the dog gets bigger, older, and stronger. Guys often seem to enjoy playing with dogs like this but it has to be eliminated, unless it is part of a specialized training process. See the Section 6 on Chewing, Toys and Play.

Massage Protocol

Desensitizing your puppy to handling can be greatly enhanced by doing regular massage. The goal is to get her to relax into the process of being touched. Remember, massage is different than play, brisk petting, or brushing.

The key is to cover **every inch** of the dog's body. Think of the massage stroke as a mother dog licking a puppy. Use enough pressure for the stroke to be comforting and go slowly enough that the dog does not get excited and want to play.

Cover every inch of the puppy. Do both sides of her mouth, over the bridge of her snout and forehead, go over both eyes, do both earflaps (carefully). Do all four legs... stroke down and slide off the paw. When the dog is comfortable with this, cradle the foot before sliding your hand off the paw. After she accepts this, stroke between the toes. And finally, stroke the pads under the feet.

Of course, stroke the main parts of the body. Go down the chest and underneath from the front, and around the rump and underneath from the back.

Do this massage daily for the first week or so with a puppy or new dog. After she is accustomed to the process and is easily relaxed, it can be done less often. I suggest doing a full body massage at least once a week—more if you like.

Do not shy away from any parts. Start in areas where the dog is less sensitive and most easily relaxed. Get the dog relaxed when stroking easily accepted parts of the body, then move to a more sensitive area, then right back to a more acceptable area. As you work with the dog, pay special attention to areas where the dog is sensitive, such as the feet and toes.

If you need to offer a special incentive for the dog to allow massage in sensitive areas, such as the feet, use a high value treat like cheese or a ball of meat. When you move to the sensitive area, put the high-value treat in front of the dog's nose and let her lick it while you stroke the area. When you move to other areas, remove the treat.

This does two things: it gives the dog something to focus on instead of worrying about the area being touched, and it also begins associating the massage with the presence of good things. This process helps build a deeper bond between you and your dog. It desensitizes your dog in her skin—makes her less reactive if touched or bumped. The process also lets you inspect the dog for bumps, bugs, burrs and sensitive areas.

Finally, it makes the dog less stressed at the veterinarian's office when being manipulated during an examination. As a byproduct, it makes life easier for your groomer.

Grooming

Different breeds and different owners have personal requirements regarding grooming. Our adult dogs are bathed and have nails trimmed and ears cleaned every four to eight weeks, depending on the individual dog's needs. Nails may need to be checked more often than during bathing, although if allowed to run outside, some dogs get dirty very quickly. Brushing should be done as needed.

If you don't want to do these things yourself, shop around for a groomer who likes dogs and with whom you are comfortable.

- Some groomers operate like an assembly line with little consideration for the animal. Other groomers truly love dogs and it shows in the way they relate to the dogs during the grooming process.

- Groomer prices vary, which is another reason to shop around. But please don't choose solely on price.

- To prepare your dog for grooming, make it a point to massage all parts of your dog's body often, checking for bugs, bumps and other potential problems.

An excellent groomer told me to make the whole grooming process predictable for the dog. That means do the same things in the same way using the same tools and the same words. If you take the dog to a groomer, try to use the same person every time. That will help the dog to be more comfortable. If you do the grooming yourself, use the same process every time.

Introducing the Bath

It's much easier to work with a puppy than to wait until you have a high-energy adolescent who wants nothing to do with a bath or nail trim. Do each of the stages suggested here on different days; don't jam it all into the day you want to give the first bath. If you are lucky, this kind of preparation can go a long way toward making the bath experience more relaxed.

- To make it easier, get the dog familiar with the grooming site using positive rewards.

- Take the dog to the tub room and give some treats.

- Put him in the tub and give some treats.

- Wet his feet and give some treats.

- Slowly work your way up the dog with water, especially if the dog is scared.

- As much as possible, connect treats with each part of the process.

With puppies, nail trims need to be started very early and done regularly. If you wait three weeks between trims, it will be like a whole new experience and may be met with resistance. Invest in a quality pair of nail trimmers and learn how to use them properly. Help the dog form a positive association with the clippers using treats, before you do any trimming at all. Then just take the very tips off one or two nails using positive reinforcement during the trim. Once that is complete, finish up matter-of-factly and the treats are put away. This way, the dog will learn that the treats are associated with the nail clippers.

A Safe House

I seldom allow our dogs to run around in the house without supervision. They spend their time in the house with me or my wife. This helps condition a dog to expected behavior.

- With a new dog, it's important to baby-proof your house just as you would for a human baby.

- Don't leave a pup unsupervised and expect things to go well. You never know when your dog will catch the scent of a dead bug that was imbedded in the stuffing of your couch when the couch was manufactured. Once the scent is identified, if the dog is bored, digging into the couch is normal behavior.

- Dogs should show consistently reliable behavior over significant time (at least a month) before they are left alone unsupervised.

- Even then, the first times alone should be short to determine how the dog will handle this new-found freedom.

- Remember, if the dog can't show behavior you want when you are with him, it's a good bet that he will not do it when you are not present.

- To leave a pup or adolescent dog loose in a house or

apartment while you are away is just asking for trouble. Consider using a crate or safe room for the dog when you must be away.

The Crate

Think of a crate as a den for your dog. A den is a cozy place that the dog can seek when she wants privacy. It also serves you when you need a break or when you will be away. If introduced properly, the dog will feel comfortable in her crate and it can be a safe place for her whole life.

To introduce the crate:

- Consider feeding your dog in the crate.

- Toss high-value treats in the crate and let the dog go in and out without closing the door.

- Hide treats in the crate for the dog to discover.

- After the dog willingly goes in and out of the crate, close the door for a few seconds, then reopen it.

- Move from a few seconds to a few minutes, then gradually to hours.

There are innumerable benefits to having a crate-trained pet. Veterinarians and groomers find crate-trained dogs much easier to care for because they are not distressed when confined to a crate. A dog crated during the night is much easier to locate and get out of the house in the event of an emergency, such as a fire. Dogs in crisis situations will often run and hide because they are frightened and won't necessarily come when called. Dogs should also be conditioned to being crated for periods when you are home or have guests.

A crate also comes in handy if you have chores to do or have guests who are afraid or don't like dogs. Or you may have guests with unruly children, and you want the dog to be protected from their ignorance. Using a special food-stuffed toy can help the dog enjoy his time in the crate and not be concerned with the visitors. Starting when the dog is young is a key to making it a part of your normal routine. This allows you to crate the dog in any situation without stress.

Section 6:
Feeding, Schedule, and Housetraining

Dog Food

Dog food is big business. Don't be fooled by heartbreaking, cute or flashy advertising. Look at the ingredients. And don't follow packaging labels to determine serving sizes for your dog. Keep in mind both the food and the treats in the volume you feed. Consult with your veterinarian to determine the healthy weight for your dog. Too much weight shortens your dog's lifespan and puts unnecessary stress on his hips and joints. The better food you feed your dog, the less volume they need, and less going in also means less coming out.

We are not nutrition experts, but we do have some experience with feeding dog food. Here is our best advice.

- When purchasing dog food, human grade ingredients are best.

- Meat should be listed first or second on the bag's ingredients list.

- Look for a superior protein source: meat or a single source meat meal such as chicken meal rather than poultry meal.

- Avoid meat by-products and generically named fats or proteins, such as animal fat and poultry fat.

- Look for whole, unprocessed grains, vegetables and other whole foods.

- Avoid food fragments such as brewers rice and corn gluten (many foods contain one of these).

- Avoid sweeteners, including corn syrup, sucrose, and ammoniated glycyrrhizin.

- Avoid propylene glycol, a moisturizer used in some foods.

The protein level of the food should also be considered. Unless you have a working dog, excess protein can give your dog excess energy that he must burn off. Without an opportunity for enough exercise, this excess energy can turn into annoying behavior in your home. We feed our large non-working dogs food with protein levels below 25%, and even less in some cases.

If you have questions about the proper protein level for your dog, consult your veterinarian or a nutrition specialist. Ask your veterinarian to show you how to evaluate your dog's fitness level. Usually it involves running your hand across the dog's rib cage and along the top of her backbone. You should be able feel her ribs without your fingers falling between them and you should be able to feel the tops of the vertebrae along her backbone. If either the ribs or the backbone are lost in a layer of fat, it's time to put the dog on a diet.

Please take care with treats as well - feeding your dog a high quality food and then using "junk food" treats would be like feeding your children organic foods and then giving them

Twinkies for dessert!

Dogs' needs change because of exercise, seasons of the year, and the amount of treats being used in their training, so measure and adjust the amount of food served accordingly.

Rituals and Housetraining

Rituals and schedules are very important in your puppy's life. They will be easier to get along with if you set regular times for exercise, meals, bed, outside time, play and so on. The more consistent the dog's schedule, the better things will go.

Since urinating and defecating are tied to eating, drinking, sleeping and exercise, your housetraining project must consider all of these. See the following sample schedule for an idea of how these things relate to one another. If you offer food and water at regular times, it will help your dog go potty at predictable times.

Most pups will need to urinate and defecate within 15 to 30 minutes after eating and drinking. Most will need to urinate immediately after waking up. Pups may need to go every hour and a half during the day.

Basically, if a dog has the opportunity, he will usually choose not to urinate or defecate where he eats and sleeps. If his quarters are too small and he is not given a chance to relieve himself outside or in another controlled area, he may have no choice.

Sample Schedule

- 6:30 a.m.: Take your pup out on leash; use a signal such as "Hurry." When the dog sniffs (looking for a spot to go), say "Good Girl." When she goes, make a fuss and give her a treat on the spot (not back in the house).

- 7:00 a.m.: Feed and water, walk pup, play with pup, return pup to crate. Pup should be confined or be with you at all times. Details on how to feed (Symbolic Feeding, a key starting point in our training system), will be detailed in Section 15.

- 10:30 a.m.: Offer water, walk pup, play 15 minutes, return to crate.

- 12:00 noon: Feed pup, offer water, walk pup, play with pup, return to crate or keep with you.

- 3:00 p.m.: Offer water, walk pup, return to crate or keep with you.

- 5:00 p.m.: Feed pup, offer water, walk pup, socialize with pup.

- 7:00 p.m.: Offer water, walk pup, play with pup, return to crate.

- 10:00 p.m.: Walk pup, return pup to crate for night.

You can develop your own schedule to match your lifestyle, but this sample gives you an idea of the approximate times and intervals between activities. Understand that at first, they are a full-time job.

If you have trouble, the first thing to evaluate is your supervision; pups should not be left unsupervised. They are like human toddlers. They will make unfortunate decisions. They do not understand the importance of your house or your possessions.

If you can't figure out why your dog is still making mistakes, tighten up your supervision and chart his eating, sleeping, exercise, drinking, urination and defecation by times of the day. Include both accidents and planned potty breaks. This kind of chart can help you understand if your dog has special potty needs.

Confine your dog to a "den" (crate) where he won't want to relieve himself. His den should be big enough to stand up, turn around in, and lie down. If the crate is bigger than this, the dog may urinate or defecate in one part of the crate and move to the other end to sleep. That defeats the purpose of using a crate for housetraining. If your dog's crate is too big, consider putting in a partition.

In addition to consistent time, use a consistent outdoor potty location. Your dog does not need a lot of room. Take him out on a six-foot leash to the same place each time. Urine smell from past visits will speed success. Use a cue to train the dog to go on command, such as "Hurry" or "Go Potty" (any simple cue will work). When you reach your chosen spot, give your cue.

When at his spot, don't play with the dog. Discourage the dog from unrelated activities. If he smells a flower, jiggle his leash and say "No, Go Potty." Use mild praise when the dog is sniffing or looking for his "spot." Use more praise and treat immediately, on the spot, when the dog has urinated or defecated.

If your dog goes in the house, only immediate intervention does any good (your voice is usually enough – an even-tempered "no-no"). Quickly interrupt the activity, then take the pup outside to finish and praise when he goes in the appropriate place. Rubbing his nose in mistakes is not effective. It may just cause the dog to do a better job of hiding the evidence. In spots where accidents have occurred, get rid of the odor quickly and completely. Use an enzyme cleaner, available at most pet supply stores. They are formulated to remove any trace of the smell, even when humans can't detect it. Learning your pup's rhythm and signals will be your best tool to prevent accidents.

Amount of Food and Water

Too much water and your dog can't hold it, too little water and he could become dehydrated. Feed and water in an area free from distractions. Put the food down for 15 or 20 minutes, then remove leftovers.

Water may be offered after eating. Allow the pup to drink all she wants in 10 minutes. The amount of water a dog needs varies due to age, activity and temperature. If you have questions about the right amount of water, talk with your veterinarian. Once a dog is housetrained, water can be available at all times.

Age of Accomplishment

Usually, pups will be housetrained by four months of age. Young pups have only partial control over their physical abilities. As they age, control increases. Supervision is critical while the dog is maturing and learning.

The Older Dog

If an older dog has a breakdown in housetraining, have your veterinarian determine if there is a physical problem. Urinary tract infections (UTIs) can cause problems for dogs in managing their urination. (Except for the increase in accidents, there may be no other sign of physical issues related to UTIs, so don't hesitate to have this checked by your veterinarian.)

If the dog is found to be healthy, consider if there has been a change in the dog's food or if the food manufacturer has changed anything in their formula or preparation. You might also want to consider a different food.

Finally, return to the methods used to originally train the dog. Be sure to restart at a level where the dog can be successful.

Section 7:
Chewing, Toys, Exercise and Play

Chewing

All dogs chew. We think chewing is one way dogs deal with anxiety. The trick is to give them things that are okay to chew. Do not give old shoes, gloves and things like that. Dogs can't tell the difference between an old shoe and a new one, so it's easier to just give them things that they can more easily identify as their toys.

- Although there is no such thing as a perfectly safe chew toy, we like nylon and rubber chew toys. They last a reasonable time and are made in different degrees of hardness, depending on how strong of a chewer your particular dog is.

- If you give your dog stuffed toys with squeakers, watch carefully because the squeakers could end up in your dog's stomach.

Check all toys carefully for safety and evaluate them against your dog's chewing capabilities.

A Cautionary Tale - One of our clients reported that they realized one of the dog's latex toys seemed to be missing. They checked the house high and low for that toy but couldn't find it. They feared the dog had eaten the toy but he didn't appear to be acting sick. They did find a portion of it in his stool one day and wondered what had happened to the rest. Still he continued to seem to be okay but a few days later (always on a weekend, to be sure) the dog was showing signs of distress, was lethargic and no longer able to go to the bathroom.

A trip to the emergency veterinary clinic revealed the remaining toy piece was creating a blockage. The client said he cried twice: Once when they told him how much they would be charging his credit card for the operation to save the dog's life, and then in joy and relief, when the vet came out of the Operating Room to say that just prior to beginning the operation, the dog had an episode of explosive diarrhea right there on the operating table and the remainder of the toy was expelled – so not only was his dog okay, but he was being given a large credit back on his card!

- If you find your pup chewing on something you don't want him to, refocus him to something you approve of and that he also likes.

- If necessary, toss a treat to divert the dog while you pick up the undesirable chew object, then give the dog something you want him to have. Be sure to praise your dog when he takes your preferred chew.

- In tough cases, you might consider using a bitter tasting spray or jelly on something you don't want the dog to chew; it may deter him.

- Be cautious when using rawhide and other recently alive chew objects. Some dogs are more likely to become possessive of these chews.

When using rawhide and the like, I suggest doing it as a

ritual. We give each dog a single roll rawhide (it holds up better) for 30 to 40 minutes each night. The dog is cued to sit, is given the roll and is then released. At the end of the allotted time, we remove the rawhide. In the early stages of teaching the dog this ritual, we tossed treats to distract the dog from the rawhide when we wanted to pick it up. Later, most dogs learn the process and relinquish the rawhide easily.

Toys in General

Dog toys are everywhere. Stuffed toys, squeaker toys, you name it—stores will sell it if people will buy it. Because toys can vary so much in how safe they are, it is a buyer beware world. Safety is a complex issue and partly depends on your dog's size, activity level and preferences. Another factor is the environment in which your dog spends time.

Although no one can guarantee a dog's enthusiasm or safety with any specific toy, there are some guidelines. The following list includes suggestions from the Dumb Friends League of Denver, Colorado.

The things usually most attractive to dogs are often the very things that are most dangerous. Dog-proof your home by safely storing string, ribbon, rubber bands, children's toys, pantyhose and anything else that could be ingested.

Avoid or alter any toys that aren't "dog proof" by removing ribbons, strings, eyes or other parts that could be chewed off and ingested. Discard toys that start to break into pieces or have pieces torn off.

Chewies (such as the rawhides mentioned above) should only be played with under your supervision. Very hard rubber toys are safer and last longer. Again, take note of any toy that contains a squeaker. Squeaking objects should be used only under your supervision.

Toys should be appropriate for your dog's size. Balls and other toys that are too small can easily be swallowed or become lodged in your dog's throat. With small dogs, I'm always surprised at how big a toy they will play with. I have seen a four-pound dog wrestle a foot-long single rolled rawhide for an hour with complete satisfaction. As long as your dog is interested and the toy presents a challenge, it's probably not too big. Most small dogs don't seem to think of themselves as small. Do some testing with the size of toys your dog likes.

Toys are not a luxury, they're a necessity. Toys help fight boredom when dogs are left alone, and toys can even help prevent some problem behaviors from developing. Dogs are often willing to play with any object they can get their paws on. That means you'll need to be particularly careful about monitoring your dog.

Active toys made of very hard material, such as Nylabone products and Kong-type products, are available in a variety of shapes and sizes and are fun for chewing and for carrying around. Rope toys are usually available in a dog bone shape with knotted ends. Tennis balls are popular dog toys, but keep an eye out for any that are chewed through and discard them. Also notice if your dog's goal is strictly to destroy toys like a tennis ball. As I mentioned, toys that can be torn to pieces and swallowed, can end up lodged in your dog's innards.

Distraction toys such as Kong-type toys, especially when they are filled with treats or a mixture of broken-up treats and peanut butter or cheese, can keep a puppy or dog busy for hours. Only by chewing diligently can your dog get to the treats, and then only in small bits.

We have also put kibble in the Kong, drizzled water over the kibble, added some cheese, put it in the freezer, and then given it to our dogs on hot days. Be sure to choose a toy that is the appropriate size for your dog.

Puzzle toys are very popular with trainers today. These toys are specifically designed to encourage a dog to use his problem-solving abilities to manipulate the toy and get the prize. They are great toys. We all know how smart our dogs can be. Thought-provoking toys help dogs build their mental abilities.

Soft stuffed toys are good for several purposes but aren't appropriate for all dogs. For some dogs, the stuffed toy should be small enough to carry around. For dogs who want to shake or "kill" the toy, it should be the size prey would be for that dog (mouse-size, rabbit-size or duck-size).

Getting the Most Out of Toys

Rotate your dog's toys weekly by making only a few toys available at a time. This makes the toy seem new to the dog. Keep a variety of types easily accessible. If your dog has a favorite, such as a soft "baby," you may want to leave it out all the time.

Provide toys that offer variety—one toy to carry, one to "kill," one to roll, and one to "baby."

Hide-and-seek is a fun game for dogs. Found toys are often much more attractive than a toy that is introduced in an obvious way. Making an interactive game out of finding toys or treats is a good rainy-day activity for your dog.

Many of your dog's toys should be interactive. Interactive play is very important for your dog because he needs active "people time." Such play also enhances the bond between you and your pet. This greatly reduces stress due to confinement, isolation and boredom. For young, high-energy and untrained dogs, interactive play also offers an opportunity for socialization and helps them learn about appropriate and inappropriate behavior.

By focusing on a specific task - such as repeatedly returning a ball, Kong or Frisbee, or playing hide-and-seek with treats or a toy - your dog can use up stored mental and physical energy in a limited amount of time and space.

All in all, play is an important part of a dog's life. As thoughtful owners, it is our job to see that play is conducted (and toys are used) in ways that end up being positive for the dog. Without our help, dogs may get into all kinds of trouble with their selection of play activities and what they choose to put into their mouth—and eventually, into their stomach.

Exercise

Dogs must have exercise to be able to relax and function as good partners. Without exercise, excess energy and anxiety may contribute to destructive or other unwanted behavior. Exercise can consist of walking, jogging, play, sports, agility or herding.

Puppies need exercise, yet shouldn't be driven to exhaustion. Length of walks should be discussed with your veterinarian as your puppy ages. Puppies should not engage in jumping where the landing will punish their soft bones and joints.

Adolescent dogs are at their physical peak. They need opportunities to get rid of their excess energy. If they don't get this opportunity, they may seem like a pestering menace... going from person to person jumping, pushing, and bumping people around.

Adult Dogs and Senior Dogs need age-appropriate exercise. Again, consult your veterinarian at your dog's annual physical examination about the appropriate level of exercise.

Generally, walking your dog is good exercise for both of you. It helps solidify the bond between you. Turning your dog loose in a back yard or at a dog park may do little to encourage exercise. Active walking and playing moving games are not only good exercise, they challenge the dog mentally. A twenty minute walk off of your property each day stimulates your dog, both physically and mentally.

Exercise needs may also be different dependent on the breed you choose. Dogs with brachycephalic (broad/short "pushed-in") faces or dogs with heavy fur coats may need special consideration in warm weather. Dogs with short coats may actually benefit from a fabric coat if walked in very cold weather. Even within a breed, the particular line (created by what breeders reinforce in their breeding) can make a difference in terms of the amount of exercise needed and the general fit in your household.

Regarding Dog Parks

Dog parks are very inviting for people who think their dog will really enjoy playing with other dogs and will get lots of good exercise in the process. While the concept appears to be a great idea, please consider that the dog park is only as good as the worst dog and the worst owner in there. It only takes a split second for something to occur between two dogs, and people put themselves at great risk breaking up a dog fight. The consequences of such a fight may be not only expensive, but heartbreaking. At the very least, choose a time when there is very little traffic at the dog park, and always have a means to leave quickly if you sense any threat.

Treadmills

A treadmill is an acceptable form of canine exercise, when it is used appropriately. We have helped clients teach their dog to walk on a treadmill. A special "dog treadmill" is not necessary; any type will do as long as the walking bed is long enough for the dog's stride and the motor and belt are smooth. As with humans, your dog should be evaluated by his doctor before starting on any strenuous exercise program. Various tips about treadmill operation are available from the suppliers.

Fetch

A game where your dog fetches an object and brings it back to you is good exercise. Some people modify the game so they can sit at the top of the stairs and toss a ball down the steps for their dog to fetch and bring back. In this kind of game, I like to use three cues: I use "Get It," "Take It" or "Fetch" as the signal to go out as I throw the object, "Bring It" is my encouragement for the dog to bring the object to me. "Drop It" is my signal to drop the object in my hand.

If the dog refuses to drop the object, I put my hand on the object and say "Drop It" again. If the dog pulls the object back in an attempt to play tug, I say "No" in a normal tone of voice and follow the dog's pull stroke (that is, I hold on but offer no resistance). At the end of the pull stroke, I again say "Drop It." not allowing the dog to make a game from his pull stroke.

I continue this sequence until the dog realizes that pulling the object is not fun without my participation. The dog never gets to have fun with the pull stoke because I don't resist, I go with it. While doing this, I am sensitive to the dog's mouth pressure on the object. As soon as I notice his mouth pressure loosening, I take the ball and say "Good Boy" (telling him he did the right thing).

In play, one of the things I take into consideration is the length of time a dog wants to play the game. I am a big believer in quitting before the dog does. If the dog will fetch eight times, I quit at five or six. That keeps the dog wanting more in the future.

Rough Play

I recommend that humans play *with* their dog, not *against* their dog. When dog owners play rough, confront their dogs, push them away, bump them, hold them down, roll them around, lie on them (and the like), they may be setting the dog up to make a mistake.

By that, I mean that the dog is being led to believe it is okay to play rough, possibly put teeth on human body parts, growl, bark and lunge at humans. Allowing or encouraging these kinds of behaviors, with even one person in the family, may set the dog up to believe that it is okay to do those behaviors with anyone. In the wrong situation, this can cost the dog her life and the human a lot of money, or worse.

I suggest that rough play between a human and a dog should only be part of a specific activity, such as a working dog sport, where the necessary safety precautions are in place. Schutzhund is an example of a working dog sport. In Schutzhund, dogs are taught to track, protect, attack on cue, escort a person in custody, conduct themselves with good manners and follow cues without hesitation.

The bottom line, in most cases, is that dogs are much tougher than humans in a pound–for–pound, one-on-one fight. That's why in sports like Schutzhund, the human in the struggle wears a heavy padded suit. When a human involves himself in rough play with his dog, the dog is in a difficult situation. The dog has to figure out how rough she can get without going too far. It's not a fair deal for the dog.

Playing Tug

A game of tug between a dog and a human has some controversial elements. Many trainers, usually those who are traditional in orientation, believe that tug brings out aggression in dogs because it encourages them to use their strength against a person. Other trainers, often more contemporary in orientation, don't believe that is necessarily true. There is also a difference of opinion about what a tug game is. One position is that it is a game that pits the owner against the dog. Another position is that the human and the dog are both beating up the tug toy.

My position is this: if you want to play tug and if your dog has not shown any aggressive tendencies so far, you can play tug if you follow the rules below. If your dog begins to show any aggressive tendencies, the tug game should stop.

Rule one: The dog only plays tug with authorized personnel. That means those who know the dog, understand the dog, and are willing to play by the rules. I recommend keeping this number small, never including strangers, and usually not including children as authorized personnel.

Rule two: Use only one tug toy and always keep it hidden away between games. This rule, combined with rule one, helps keep the dog focused on the game. When you are ready to play tug, you and the dog go to the storage place and get the toy.

Rule three: You get the game going. As you play, you should win about half the time. If necessary, you can teach the dog an "Out" cue to let her know she should let go of the toy. Teaching **"Out"** involves signaling the dog with a verbal or other cue that she should release the toy. To do this, stop resisting the dog's tugging, show the dog a treat and say "Out." Usually, if the treat is of high value to the dog, she will release the tug toy and take the treat. You say "Good Girl" and then ask the dog to sit. If she sits, you say "Good Girl, Okay," and restart the tug game.

Rule four: On several occasions when you are in possession of the tug toy, you should ask the dog to do a simple task, such as sit. If the dog does sit, she is telling you two things. One is that she is not so agitated that she can't comply with your behavior cue. The other is she is willing to comply with your request. If the dog complies, you say "Good Girl, Okay," and restart the tug game. If the dog *can* not or *will* not comply with your simple cue, you say "Too Bad" and put the tug toy away. You can try again a few hours later or the next day.

Rule five: The dog's teeth must never touch your skin. If they do, you instantly say "Too Bad" and put the tug toy away. The phrase "Too Bad" is used as a marker to signal the dog that the associated behavior results in the end of the game.

Rule six: Remember - don't leave the tug toy out when you are done with the game. Put it back in storage.

Rule seven: Don't play tug with any other toy.

These rules help prevent you from setting your dog up for a mistake.

Section 8:
Multiple Dog Families

Having first lived with a loosely associated neighborhood dog pack, then with a single dog for 15 years, then with three, five and as many as 24 dogs (14 adults and 10 puppies) when I was active in breeding, I can testify that there are major differences as you increase the family dog population.

The multiple behaviors that must be dealt with as one adds a second, third or more dogs can be overwhelming. The problem is further magnified by inaccurate and inappropriately applied wolf research that suggests all wolves live in harmony under the supervision of a confident pack leader.

It is an erroneous belief that dogs are pack animals, just like wolves. Many presume that dogs should get along in any home pack environment we impose, as long as there is an alpha (human or canine) to keep things under control, but this is a recipe for some serious problems.

When I am contacted by someone who wants help with a multiple dog problem, I always take a deep breath and wonder how realistic the person's perspective will be. Sometimes the problem can be resolved, at other times, not in the way the owner thinks it should.

Dogs vs. Wolves

The best presentation of this issue that I have seen was given

Dogs As Family Members

by Temple Grandin in her book ***Dogs Make Us Human, Chapter 2*** (2009). She presents research noting that **wolves live in small well controlled family packs.** They establish their own territory and rarely take in outsiders.

Over their lives, wolves learn both aggressive and submissive behaviors. Aggressive behaviors are learned first so that puppies and adolescents are able to protect themselves if attacked. As wolves mature, they learn submissive behaviors that can be used to save their lives if confronted by a bigger stronger wolf. With wolves, it is a *family* relationship where learning both aggressive and submissive behaviors makes it possible for the pack to work.

This is not the way it is with dogs. Grandin reports that when dogs were put into simulated pack situations, things did not go well. It seems that the dogs had not developed the submissive behaviors needed to negotiate a family-like relationship with peers.

From Grandin's perspective, all this leads to the conclusion that "anyone who has more than two dogs better know what they are doing." Humans seem to want to put any assortment of dogs together in a family structure, sometimes in very small spaces, and figure the dogs should just get along.

The reality is, we cannot count on the dogs to just get along. Putting two dogs together can be a crap shoot. Litter mates are even more of a crap shoot. Putting big dogs with tiny dogs is not only a crap shoot, it can be a death sentence to the smaller dog (if only by an accidental paw-shot to the spine delivered in fun). Even when two dogs get along for years that is not to say that things will not change. A younger dog may all of a sudden decide she can take the older dog. Then, a bump at the wrong time when one dog doesn't feel good can be the trigger.

Please. Don't be naïve and put dogs in an imposed pack with no human management and expect all to go well. Imposed packs need to be carefully built and managed. If they are not, in time, the result can be heartbreaking. Think carefully what dogs you will put together, and about how you will manage things if you see a problem forming.

When introducing a new dog into the household it is crucial to have a plan; to do otherwise is foolish. If you don't know how to handle this type of situation, seek the advice of a professional *before* you risk setting the dogs up to fail.

What About Siblings?

Complicating the multi-dog family, are sibling relationships. Brothers and sisters add just one more dimension that must be dealt with. What often happens here is that a would-be pet owner goes to a breeder or rescue organization looking for a companion. On their search, they find the cutest dog... who has been kept with his brother or sister. What happens next is: "I couldn't bear to separate them," so both dogs go to the new home.

Now begins the saga. If siblings have been kept together, they can develop what I might call a dysfunctional relationship. (Think of how human twins often get in far more trouble together, than age-mixed siblings) This starts because they have likely been together since birth. If they're always kept together, they may not have developed independently. One may have counted on the other to do the exploring while he or she held back. In general, they may be more dependent on each other than is good when you are trying to make them a part of your family.

What sometimes seems true is that siblings spend time undoing the things that humans want to teach them so they can be good pets. To combat this, I recommend that owners consciously work to develop an *individual* relationship with each sibling. Be sure each dog gets individual play time and individual training time. Provide enough separation that each can develop an independent personality. Work through the structure suggested in this book with each dog. If you do these things, you have a good chance to head off potential problems.

If someone asks us ahead of time, we would definitely recommend that they *not* purchase two puppies at the same time from the same litter. Sadly, breeders may not raise or even know of the problems that are potentially present, and will often encourage would-be buyers to take that second equally cute pup.

A better strategy, if you know you want two dogs. is to adopt one. First establish a good training and behavior structure with this one, *then* add that second dog to your family. Repeat the behavior program and spend time separately playing and training the new pup while also paying attention to your older one.

Section 9:
Two Schools of Thought

At this point you may have noticed, in what I have shared about training, that punishment is not my favored general training paradigm. As you hear more from me you may find yourself thinking, "I would just swat Fido," and that would be the end of it. As you move forward I ask you to hold your judgment until you hear more of the story.

Let me describe some of the main schools of thought about dog training as I see them, so you can understand where I ended up.

The Traditional Approach

For over 100 years, the traditional approach of, "praise when Rover does well, and punish when he does wrong," has been the accepted norm.

This punishment runs the full gamut from a stern word, to a swat, to forcefully holding a dog down, to using a choke collar, electric shock, and even death, if a dog does not correct.

Traditional training can work if it is done skillfully by a well-trained handler. Far more often, I have seen it done incorrectly, with poor timing, too harshly (or not harsh enough), and at the loss of a good relationship between the owner and the dog.

My father-in-law would be an extreme case in point. He was a farmer. His approach to dog training was to bring a dog home, (usually a dog that someone had given him), turn him loose, and hope he would do the right things… i.e. guard the farm, leave farm animals alone, and not bite visitors. If the dog made a mistake he was punished, tied up on a chain, or worse.

If these are the methods you grew up with and which you believe work, and if you are not open to change, then this is not the book for you.

The Contemporary Approach

I have chosen (and succeeded in using) the contemporary approach that has emerged from animal research in the recent decades, and which revealed that using **positive motivation** makes much more sense and has fewer downsides than punishment.

The cost of losing a warm relationship with my pet through punishment is not a price I am usually willing to risk paying. Perhaps, even more foundationally, "Why would I use punishment on my loyal companion, when there are other effective ways to train her?"

By way of example, I once worked with a 4-H member who was doing the initial training of a dog who would eventually become a service dog. The 4-H'er had done this before and had a plan about how to proceed. I came into the picture because the organization that would eventually train the dog for service work, wanted the dog to have some formal obedience training.

What I noticed immediately, was that whenever this young handler gave a cue to the dog, the dog would wince, back up, duck or shy away. It became clear that the dog was expecting to be "hurt" if he didn't know or perform the action being requested of him. This was the training method taught to the young handler in that particular 4-H club. (4-H clubs vary in the training methods used.)

When I asked the young man why the dog reacted this way, his response was one of confusion. When I suggested that the dog was worried about being punished, there was even more confusion. The befuddlement declined as we worked with the dog using rewards when cues were completed. He witnessed the warmth of relationship that could be cultivated with the dog, while still achieving training goals. This example points out the transition stage that dog training is in.

The Extremes

Being what some would call a *crossover trainer* (meaning I started training in the 1950s when the traditional approach was pretty much it), I am well aware of the extremes that can exist in either of these training approaches.

The extreme traditional trainer will use almost any level of force to get compliance from the dog—anything, including strangling with a choke chain or pinch collar, shocking various parts of the body, pinning the dog to the ground, swatting the dog with various implements, even swinging the dog in circles off the ground to subdue him. Sounds pretty horrible, doesn't it? Remember, this is the *extreme* traditional trainer.

The extreme contemporary trainer may believe a dog should never experience stress of any kind. At this extreme, some contemporary trainers might even allow a dog to be euthanized rather than use methods that would be considered aversive (involving discomfort) as part of a behavior modification plan.

I have known owners who feed their dogs homemade meals made up of roast beef, veggies and maybe even dessert. They respond to their dog's every whim, often because the dog is in a constant state of whining, leaning on the owner, pushing with her head, nudging, pawing, or barking demandingly. In some cases people are literally feeding their dog to death and creating an environment where there are no expectations placed on the dog in exchange for the relationship with the human.

When the situation becomes intolerable, help is sought— perhaps because the dog has bitten someone or attacked another dog and the owner realizes the dog could be taken away. Other times it is because the dog will not get off the bed, will not come when called, refuses to walk on a leash, goes potty in the house...and the list goes on.

When help is finally sought, the problem is complicated by the fact that the dog has experienced few expectations regarding his behavior and the owner wants the problem solved without any changes in the dog's life. More to the point, he doesn't want to ask the dog to comply with anything in order to live in partnership with a human, yet behavior changes are desired.

The owner may tell me that the dog is not "food motivated"

or will not work for food. In some of these cases, just one look at the "plumpkin" in question and you know why. The reality for me is that I have never found a dog who is not food-motivated if the conditions are right.

Dogs Form Preferences

Believe me when I tell you that the choices you make will impact your relationship with your dog. I have had numerous experiences witnessing dogs expressing their preference by the people they choose to be with.

Those experiences reinforce our advocacy for a training approach that not only produces good behavior, but which *bonds* the dog with us as well.

Your Choice

You need to spend some time assessing your own history and bias regarding dog training, and then choose your trainer and the particular method you feel you can use with your companion.

Ask questions, read printed material, interview trainers, and (if practical) *watch them at work* to be sure you know what you are in for. Ask around about a particular trainer's reputation. **Ask enough questions so that you feel comfortable.** If a trainer seems defensive about your questions regarding his approach, a red flag should go up.

If you are willing to explore the positive reinforcement training protocol, you will find good material here. It is a good idea to read through the remainder of the book before beginning to train. That way you will understand the destination, and how the elements fit into a whole.

I have gone to great lengths to be detailed in my explanations. I have also stated on several occasions that if the things I suggest do not seem to work for you, please get help from a certified trainer or behavior expert. If things are not working, there is a possibility that you may be misinterpreting my writing or that your personal bias is pushing you in a different direction than I intended. Please don't take this as a criticism, it happens to all of us at one time or another.

It is also possible that your dog requires additional support beyond what I can put in this book. In any case, don't despair; just get help from a qualified source. And don't be surprised if the help you seek does not do things exactly the way I might. As I noted earlier, there are a lot of paths to the same solution.

My Bottom Line

Everyone has a bias about how things should be done. Mine is that animals are living beings and deserve to be treated with respect and dignity. At the same time, it seems unrealistic to me that any animal can live with no stress in his or her life. Consider your own life: is every day a bundle of joy? Do you never wonder or worry about what is coming next? Are you never startled, never concerned, never afraid?

If you are like me, you experience all these things. And if you are like me, what you hope is that you will be able to handle them and keep functioning in ways that guarantee your success and satisfaction. Likewise, I work with dogs knowing that some stress is bound to come into their lives, and I want them equipped to handle it. The very existence of stressors, provides opportunities to train and reinforce good choices.

Section 10:
Options for Training

Some dog owners believe that, if training is even necessary, the best option is to attend a training class consisting of six to eight group lessons. In those classes, a dog should be taught obedience commands.

For others, dog training is a series of classes at different levels. Each level is designed to teach more difficult concepts, leading to competition in shows or trials that showcase the dog's abilities. For most of us, dog training is a process through which we develop a satisfying relationship with a loved companion.

As I mentioned in the last section, a great deal of research has been done that has influenced the methods trainers use. These new methods have had a profound impact on both training approaches and the environment in which training takes place. There are a variety of approaches that enable trainers and behavior professionals to be more skillful in matching their strategies to the needs of the dog and the values of the owner.

The success of any training program depends on the amount of effort the owner is willing and able to put forth. Make no mistake, good behavior does not occur without effort, and changing the behavior of a problem dog requires even more effort.

The cost of training depends on how far you want to go. Typical options include a basic evaluation, participation in group classes, individual private lessons at a training center, a trainer coming to your home, or you can even send your dog away for in-kennel training. In this section, we'll discuss each of these options.

When to Begin Training

About ten weeks of age is a good time to begin training.

Between four and six months of age, as the young dog moves into adolescence, independence-seeking becomes a focus. This independent stage may last for a year or longer, depending on the size and breed of dog. Adolescence is a time when clear communication and training is a must to minimize frustration for both dog and human. The earlier this training starts, the better for both.

Here are the primary options currently available:

Puppy School

Most puppy classes include basic instruction, socialization activities and games to help develop agility and confidence. Check with your veterinarian about how old your pup should be before she meets other dogs at a puppy class. Usually, a 10- to 12-week-old puppy can go to class if she is up-to-date on her inoculations.

Group Classes

Group obedience classes have typically been the most widely

available. In a group class, you buy a package of six to eight sessions that are about 50 minutes each. In group sessions, help with individual problems and setting up the right structure for home is difficult because of time constraints. The advantage of group sessions is that a dog gets to experience learning in a dynamic social environment.

Instructors for these classes may come from several sources. Professional Trainers are those who train to earn a living, Club Trainers are those who train as a hobby, and there are other types of self-designated trainers. The credentials of trainers vary widely.

We have offered several types and levels of small group classes, depending on the skill and interest of the dog/handler team. To ensure that the dog will benefit from a class and be safe in a group, we usually start by working with the dog individually. There may be from one to four or more individual private sessions, depending on the dog. Dogs with severe problems may require a number of individual sessions along with gradual introduction into a specialty group, such as a class for reactive dogs. From a specialty group, the dog may progress into more general obedience or agility groups.

Private Lessons

Private lessons offer an individualized approach. They are usually done with an individual owner, a family or with one or two other people with similar goals. In private lessons, a dog's specific problems can be diagnosed and strategies can be designed to manage or alleviate them. During our private consultations, a structure for living in the human household is established.

Basic behavior commands or cues are put in place and family members are taught how to train their dog, solve problems and manage or prevent difficult situations. In this format, everything is done one-on-one. And one of the biggest benefits is that trainers get to know the client and his dog on a much more personal level. Most people are interested in having a well-mannered pet; and in today's culture it is wise to have an interest in safety and liability as well.

Training in Your Home

If you are unable to leave your home due to illness or because you cannot travel, you may want to consider in-home training. Basically, you will be paying for private lessons plus a travel fee (for mileage and time spent on the road).

Some believe that a dog with problems is best trained in the home where the behavior is displayed. Our experience is that training may be more effective when the dog is brought to us to be assessed and receive his basic training. We can help his humans set up a behavior modification plan. Then, when the dog goes back to the home and the problem comes up, the owner has a specific plan for what to do and has had practice using proper techniques.

The neutral environment, away from home, gives the owner the ability to see their dog in a different light. This is conducive to learning new ways of approaching problems and building relationship. Many of our clients, some who even initially thought they wanted in-home training, have commented on the advantages of meeting away from the home.

In-Kennel Training

In-kennel training means your dog stays with a trainer for a period of time ranging from one or two weeks up to a few months. If you are interested in training with the least personal involvement, perhaps because you don't have the time, are unable to do the work, a special skill is needed, or your dog has a serious problem, this type of training might be for you.

In this training format, the professional trainer works with your dog several times a day to teach a set of behaviors that have been specified in a contract. After the residential period, the trainer teaches the owner what the dog has been trained to do and how to keep the dog working at home. For this method to be successful, the owner must follow the instructions set out by the kennel trainer. If the owner does not follow through, the dog will become lax in her training.

Anyone who is considering this approach should do so with great care. You must be absolutely sure of the training methods that will be employed with your dog and the safety of the facility.

Make Sure Your Trainer is a Good Fit

When you're looking for a trainer, the most important things to consider are - can you live with the methods used with your pet and can you feel comfortable with the individual you are working with? If the answer to either of these is no, you are likely to be uncomfortable about the way your dog is treated.

The best way to make decisions about a trainer is to read the written material they put out and talk with them either in person or by phone (e-mail may also work). Ask questions about the things that concern you and that will be factors in your comfort.

Keep in mind the earlier discussion of traditional versus contemporary trainers, and the substantially different approaches they may use. Take the time and look carefully at all prospective trainers, and explore their methods thoroughly.

When talking with trainers, any question is fair game as long as you are polite. If a prospective trainer or behavior consultant acts as if you should not be asking a particular question, that is reason for caution on your part.

Locating Trainers

To find trainers in your area, the following web sites may be helpful. Each of the groups listed here has been in existence long enough to have obtained credibility for what they offer and each has a trainer locater on its website.

Just look for the locator and follow the directions to type in either a zip code or postal information, and you will be given a list of trainers in your area. Those designated as Certified Trainers have been trained in a specific curriculum. Some research into the nature of the curriculum may be of value as you search for the trainer that matches your needs.

- **International Association of Animal Behavior Consultants (www.iaabc.org):** this organization's membership has a contemporary orientation and focuses on behavior analysis and modification. Members are behavior consultants.

- **Certification Council for Professional Dog Trainers (www.CCPDT.org):** an organization that tests and certifies professional dog trainers.

- **Association of Pet Dog Trainers (www.apdt.com):** an education, support and training organization of contemporary, reinforcement-based dog trainers.

- **International Association of Canine Professionals (www.dogpro.org):** members of this organization represent a cross section of dog training.

- **National K-9 Trainers (www.nk9dta.com):** this organization trains and certifies trainers in all facets of dog training.

Just remember, there is no single national or state agency for licensing or certifying dog trainers or behavior professionals and there are no uniform certification standards. Various universities, specialty schools and other organizations provide programs and certify graduates. Methods vary greatly. Because there is no uniform trainer certification standard, anyone can declare him or herself a dog trainer, so it's important to carefully consider the credentials (and track record) of those you may choose as guides for you and your dog.

Building Your Home Training Team

When you're ready to start, you need to build a training team. This is different than picking a trainer. I generally suggest that anyone who lives in your home, as well as anyone who comes to your home frequently, should be considered as a part of your training team. These are the people who will make a difference in how your dog will be trained. It's very important that you know who *is* and who *is not* part of that team. Here are two criteria those on your team must meet:

1. **Members of your training team must be *willing* to do what you ask** when interacting with your dog. That means you have a responsibility to make sure they agree to help in the ways you ask, and that they will learn the proper way to interact with your dog. You must get this commitment, and you must teach them what to do, or you must include them in the training process with your trainer so they can learn firsthand.

2. **Members of your training team must be *capable* of doing what you ask** when interacting with your dog. This means physically and mentally capable. You could have a 90-year-old grandmother who is willing but not capable. You could have a 15-year old who is capable but not willing. It is your responsibility to make this assessment.

The reason for these criteria is that if you are working hard to teach your dog a desired behavior, and someone else allows the dog to practice an incompatible and undesired behavior, your efforts will be seriously hampered and your training plan undermined.

If you are trying to teach your dog not to jump up, you want everyone the dog comes in contact with to practice interaction that will discourage jumping. If someone says, "It's okay, I like it when dogs jump up to greet me" and then allows the dog to jump on him, that person is working against you and your training program.

In dealing with those who won't or can't do what you ask when interacting with your dog, you must take control of the situation so that the dog will not be allowed to practice behaviors you don't want. If necessary, you may want to keep the dog on leash or in a crate in the presence of those people.

And please don't forget to reinforce your dog for keeping four feet on the floor! Whatever we reinforce - either purposely or by accident - will grow stronger. It is important that we pay attention and take advantage of those times we can strengthen behaviors we like.

You May Have to Get Tough

If you have small children, they may not be willing or in some cases able, to do what is necessary and safe to interact properly with your dog. You have to decide what they will be allowed and not allowed to do. You may also have to set ground rules with young children: For example: "If you run and the dog chases you around the house, you will not be able to play with the dog."

I know this might sound harsh, but it is inappropriate behavior on the part of children that can end in a nip or bite, and then be interpreted as bad behavior on the dog's part.

Good old Uncle George may also be a problem. When Uncle George comes over, does he encourage your dog to jump on him or get on the furniture? If he does, and if those are behaviors you don't want, you've got to either teach Uncle George what to do or, if he is not willing to cooperate, be sure you are in control of the dog when your uncle comes to your house.

I know issues like this can be sensitive in settings with family and friends. Your job is to figure out how to pull it off without offending anyone. Remember, you can always blame it on your trainer... or the author of this book.

Section 11:
Collars and Leashes

Listed below is the typical equipment our clients have seen being used in the dog world at large. I make it a point to educate clients about equipment and its uses (even things we would never recommend and why).

We prefer working with a six-foot leash and a flat collar. If the dog is a larger breed, we like the old-fashioned buckle collar because we think it is the most secure. When working on leash walking, we encourage work with a flat collar first to see how much progress can be made. If progress is not as desired, we move to power steering devices.

I have listed several types of power steering devices. These help keep the dog from pulling while learning. One we favor is a specially designed chest harness which has a front leash clip at chest level. These harnesses are usually accepted by the dog without much fuss. The head harness is my preference for a dog who pulls and throws in a lot of head action. It works well and usually requires about a 20-minute process to begin desensitizing the dog.

Leashes and Long Lines

Leather, nylon, cotton, chain cable and rubber-coated materials are used for leashes, lines and tethers. We like leather as a training leash because of its positive, comfortable feel in the hands. But remember, never leave leather alone with your dog or it will likely become a chew toy. Nylon is strong but not as comfortable in your hands.

Occasionally, we suggest nylon-coated cable as a drag line or tether for a puppy who chews. Cotton lines are comfortable, light and less durable than nylon. Chain should be avoided as a leash. Parachute cord is great for long lines. A six-foot leash is usually used to begin training and it allows enough length to work away from the dog as he improves.

Harness

A harness is sometimes used because owners believe that a dog will choke himself on a neck collar. Unless specifically designed as a walking control harness, dogs may actually pull harder when a traditional harness is used. The Easy Walker and Halti Harness are specially designed to get a less agitating walk.

Head Halter

Two common head halter brands are Halti and Gentle Leader. They are applied to the snout and head like a horse halter. They are effective because they provide maximum leverage and head control for the handler. Head control can be an issue with reactive or aggressive dogs. Dogs may fuss about having something on their snout and desensitization is usually required. An instructional video may come with the head halter to teach you how to desensitize your dog.

Flat Collar

Flat collars are generally considered a safe and humane tool for leash walking or tethering a dog. They have plastic clips or metal buckles and are usually made of leather or nylon. This is the only collar I would consider leaving on my dogs when I am not with them.

Limited Slip Collar

Sometimes called a Martingale collar or Greyhound collar, the partial slip collar can be made of nylon, chain or both. This collar is sometimes used because of the limited slip feature, which helps prevent dogs from slipping the collar (when they have a big neck and narrow head). They may help with control, too, but stop short of allowing the handler to choke the dog.

Slip or "Choke" Collar

These are available in chain of variable size links, as well as in nylon and leather. Slip collars are often called "choke" collars" because, if used inappropriately, the dog can be choked. Dogs should never be tethered by a slip collar and slip collars should not be left on unsupervised dogs.

There is a correct and an incorrect way to wear and use a slip collar. Sadly, this collar is often put on and/or used incorrectly. Most people seem to believe that this collar is designed so that when the dog pulls, he chokes himself and that stops him from pulling. This is not correct. The slip collar is a difficult tool for most handlers to use and it is usually associated with the use of punishment as a training technique.

Prong or "Good Dog" Collar

Made with metal or plastic prongs on the inside and somewhat ominous looking, these collars close slightly when the leash is pulled. This causes a pinching effect. Some people believe this collar mimics a mother dog's teeth as used to discipline puppies. These collars are sometimes used for dogs who need a form of "power steering."

Prong collars can be misused and are often seen as undesirable. In spite of their appearance, these collars are still used in training some assistance dogs. When they are used, they are often seen as a way to help neutralize the physical strength of the dog versus a person with a handicap or someone who needs support because of their age.

Electronic Collars

Variations of these collars use sprays, vibrations, audible signals or electric shock as ways to affect behavior. Some of these may be useful when appropriately matched to specific behavior circumstances, under proper supervision.

It is not appropriate to buy an electric collar and start shocking a dog when he does something "wrong." A clear behavior strategy should be used with any of these tools. In some cases, these collars can make behavior worse.

If the dog associates a shock with a particular person or

classification of people (such as children), the dog may become more anxious or aggressive around them. Dogs can even seem to become "schizophrenic" with misuse of these devices.

Extreme caution is recommended. Do not use these devices without help from a certified trainer or behavior consultant. If you are told by one of these people that you should not be using this kind of device, I would follow the recommendation.

Section 12:
Groundwork: Basic Stuff

Now that we've covered puppy basics, the nature of dogs and humans, and options for training and basic equipment, allow me to introduce my method.

As you enter our training facility, you are greeted by the trainer or behavior consultant assigned to you. In many cases that person is me, Jim—also known as Dr Jim, Uncle Jim or Your Friend Jim as the dogs get to know me.

Your first chore, if not done previously, is to complete a behavior history and a liability waiver. The behavior history tells me details about your experiences with your dog so far. It helps me understand the context for your dog's behavior.

Our Liability Waiver

Our liability waiver, which we referenced in this book's disclaimer, is reproduced on the following pages. It is intended to be thorough and will give you a sober education about dog ownership.

Waiver and Release

I. Participant Information _____

II. Liability Release

In consideration for Signature K-9 Behavior and Training LLC, Northern Legend Kennel and/or James or Charlene Akenhead allowing me, my spouse, or my child (or children) or those for whom I am guardian, and/or pets to participate in activities such as those described herein, I agree as follows:

1. This agreement, waiver and release apply to Northern Legend Kennel, Signature K-9 Services, James and Charlene Akenhead, as well as any committees, employees, predecessors, successors, attorneys, insurers, as well as members, volunteers, officers, trustees, sponsors, shareholders or board of directors of any group or organization (all of these are identified below as "Released Parties") who are working in the scope of their duties at the time of occurrence of any omission which is later alleged to be a cause or contribution to a claim for injury, damages or death.

2. I forever release, hold harmless and indemnify Released Parties from any and all liability, claims, suits, costs and attorneys, causes of action, damages, injuries or death to me, my minor children, any children under my supervision, my dog(s), my property, and legal liability of every nature, including negligent acts or omissions of any Released Parties, whether known or unknown, anticipated or unanticipated, direct or indirect, arising out of participation in the past, present, or future activities (including, but not limited to, activities such as visiting for entertainment;

selection of a puppy, dog, or rescued dog; purchasing a dog; providing work or service in the kennel or with kenneled animals; while training my dog(s) or dogs belonging to others; while assessing dogs; while playing with dogs; while grooming dogs; when boarding dogs; or for any other activity). I assume all risks of injury or death as set forth in this release.

3. It is my express intent that this Waiver and Release shall bind the members of my family, my spouse, and my estate, as well as my heirs, administrators, personal representatives, or assigns, and shall be deemed as a Release and Waiver, Discharge and Covenant not to sue the above-named Released Parties, even if they engage in negligent conduct: and I make this agreement, Waiver and Release on behalf of myself, my spouse, my child and/or heirs, executors, administrators, successors, representatives and assigns.

III. Activity Risk
I understand that those involved in supervising or assisting with activities may not be professionals. I also understand that when working with or being around dogs there are numerous obvious and non-obvious inherent risks of serious injury or death, or property damage, to me or my dog, or others, which are always present in the type of activities noted herein. I acknowledge the information noted in section IV. Nature of Dogs, and understand that I am solely responsible for assessing my ability and confidence to participate in any activity and that I may decline to participate in any activity.

IV. Nature of Dogs
Although dogs are often thought of as honorable, loyal and trustworthy companions, I also understand that dogs, irrespective of training, may react unpredictably at times,

based upon instinct or circumstances, including but not limited to: reaction to sounds, movements, unfamiliar objects, persons or animals; certain hazards such as surface and subsurface conditions; collisions with other dogs, handlers, or objects; participant negligence; as well as unpredictable or erratic actions by others and may become fierce, aggressive, vicious, or dangerous and may attack people without warning. Further, it is recognized that any dogs present may not have received required or recommended vaccinations and that this represents additional danger of injury or death to my dog(s). Additional risks from dogs include, but are not limited to: dog fights, dog bites and injuries to humans and other dogs; dog theft or unlawful capture; dog escape over or under fences or through doors; plants and/or water sources; vegetation that may have burrs or seeds that could become tangled in a dog's coat or lodge in a dog's feet, ears, nose, or eyes; mosquitoes, ticks, chiggers, fleas or other insects, wild animals such as skunks, raccoons, opossums or stray dogs.

I also acknowledge that dogs may fail to respond to cues or commands; they may escape, or slip their collar; that dogs are faster than humans and may bite, change direction or speed, trip, slip, fall, stop short, shift weight, spook, or run if danger is perceived or if frightened. provoked, or for no obvious reason whatsoever. Finally, I understand that serious injury or death may result from working with or being around dogs.

V. Conditions and Nature of Locations
Released Parties have not inspected, and make no warranties concerning the safety or condition of any surface, site, building or other location of events or activities, including those in a private home.

VI. Emergency Treatment

I agree that the Released Parties are granted permission to authorize emergency medical treatment and I agree that I am solely responsible for payment of any such medical treatment. I also understand that the Released Parties assume no responsibility for any injury or damage which might arise out of or in connection with such authorized emergency medical treatment.

I have read, understand and voluntarily agree *to this four-page waiver and release. I further agree that no oral statements, representations or inducements apart from this written agreement have been made to obtain my consent. I further agree that this waiver, release and covenant not to sue shall remain in effect until revoked in writing by me. I also agree that should I revoke this waiver, release and covenant not to sue, I will no longer be able to participate in activities of the type represented herein and that the provisions of this agreement shall remain in effect as described for any and all activities or consequences of activities in which I have participated up to the date of the revocation.*

Participant's Signature _____

If participant is under 18, *the signature of parent or legal guardian signifies and represents agreement to the terms of this waiver, release and covenant not to sue on behalf of the minor and, if applicable per the specifications of participation noted herein, to him or herself.*

The Complexity of Liability

The liability issue is complicated. The waiver was designed after research into a variety of organizations and was reviewed by our attorney before we put it into use.

The bottom line here is that dogs are living beings. There are no guarantees about their behavior - any more than there are guarantees about human behavior. The news is full of stories of individuals who seemed like normal quiet neighbors one day, who snapped and went on a killing spree the next. Behavior and its roots are complex.

People need to be aware that there are no guarantees, and that their personal commitment is going to be necessary, if their companion is to become their partner in a solid relationship.

A Caution

I have had the good fortune to attend several seminars by Dr. Pamela Reid. At one of those seminars, Dr. Reid presented video case studies of dog behavior evaluations. In one case, everyone in the room fell in love with the dog in the video. The dog couldn't be nicer. He did everything right. The situation was a set-up.

This was a model dog who was tested in all kinds of activities, and had a perfect evaluation. The audience was shocked to learn that later, when he was away from the evaluation setting, this dog attacked someone. He had such a severe reaction to a particular trigger that he had to be euthanized.

Dr. Reid's point, I believe, was that there is no foolproof evaluation system. My translation is that you can test a dog on 100 things; he may pass the first 99 and trigger at the 100th. For that reason, we must understand that we have a big responsibility when we take on a canine companion. Also for that reason, I can *not* do an evaluation after a dog has bitten and assure the owner - or a court - that it will not happen again.

Even so, many situations can be managed. That means a structure for life (which, if it had existed in the beginning, would likely have prevented the bite), a clear set of cues, behavior markers that have been carefully taught, and a commitment to make the plan work. In these cases, the future is really in the hands of the owner or handler of the dog. It can't be left up to the dog with the idea that if he is "trained," nothing will go wrong. The owner dare not become lackadaisical after months or even years of uneventful success.

Getting to Know Your Dog

While you complete the required forms at our training facility, I get to know your dog by walking her around the facility, letting her look in the corners and behind the desk to be sure there are no boogey men hiding in wait. (If the dog is scared or wants to bite me, I forgo this activity.)

During this exploration, I toss treats on the floor to see how the dog reacts. If the dog readily picks up the treats and looks to me for more, I suspect that the socialization process is on the right track. If the dog shies away, won't eat a treat, carries herself low or won't go with me at all, I begin to assume that socialization may need work. Usually, there is time for me to test the dog to see if she will follow a lure into various positions. This is early preparation for teaching cues.

The Interview

After I get to know your dog, I get to know you. The process begins as I ask for an overview of the situation. I take notes about major issues and compare client comments with information on the assessment sheet that has been completed.

My questions are often phrased as, "Exactly how, when, where, and with whom does this behavior take place?" My goal is to get precise details about the behavior and its context. Without these details, it is difficult to come up with a good plan.

Protocol: A Structure for Doing Things

Armed with all this basic information, I establish a training protocol for this family, making sure all specific problems identified by the dog's owner are accounted for. Often, at least some of the owner's problems are resolved as we put my basic framework in place. Later, when assessing how things are going, I recheck against the protocol, because I often find that if problems continue, some part of the original protocol is not being followed.

For example, my protocol includes a process to stop jumping. It also involves a specific feeding process that helps establish various roles in the family. It supports everything else that we do. If a client tells me she is not using the feeding protocol, she has removed one of the support systems of my approach.

If a client tells me the dog won't stop jumping, I ask how she reacts to this jump. If she says, "I tell him to stop," I know there is a problem because, that is not part of my protocol.

If the protocol *is* being followed as explained, and the behavior continues, we work more on problem solving to find the weak link.

Section 13:
The Thinking Behind Our Training

Following is the foundation we make sure clients understand before we begin.

Explanation of Approaches

In a private training session, the first thing you hear from me is an overview of training methodologies mentioned earlier.

Clients quickly come to understand that my inclination is to use positive motivation as much as is possible. My way of stating this is**, "We teach the dog that to get what she wants, she must give us what we want. We do that with a focus on rewarding behaviors we** *want* **rather than punishing behaviors we** *don't want."*

Positive Reinforcement

Positive reinforcement means giving your pet something pleasant immediately after she does something you want her to do. That pleasant experience makes the dog more likely to do the behavior again. For best results, the pleasant experience (the reward) should show up within a couple of seconds after the behavior you want. For example, if you ask your dog to sit and the pleasant experience happens after she stands back up, she'll think she's being rewarded for standing up. She won't make the connection with the sit. This shows how timing your reward makes a difference in how easily and quickly the dog learns.

Positive reinforcement, your timely reward, can be anything the dog likes, including food treats, praise, petting, going outside, a drink of water, a favorite toy or a game.

Food Treats

Food treats usually work well when training your dog. Food is what is called a primary reinforcer. That means you don't have to teach the dog to like it. You just have to find a food treat that the dog values.

Your training treat should be a small piece of soft food, so that your dog can immediately get it down and look to you for more. If you give her something she has to chew or that breaks into bits and falls on the floor, she'll be looking on the floor, not at you.

Small pieces of soft commercial treats, hot dogs, cheese, cooked chicken or beef, all work well. Each time you use a food reward, you should pair it with a verbal signal (praise)... something like "Good Dog" in a positive, happy tone of voice. You could also reinforce the behavior with a toy or brief play. The reason I prefer food for initial training is that it's easier.

When you're teaching a new behavior, your dog should be rewarded each time she does the behavior. This continuous delivery of reinforcement should be used until your dog associates the cue you use with the position you are cuing and the name (sound) you give it.

Literally anything the dog likes that is okay with the owner can be used to reinforce a behavior. When using food, all you have to do is figure out what food the dog likes and you are holding all the cards. The value of all treats or rewards is decided by the dog.

You might think giving Cheerios is a great treat. Most dogs probably won't see it that way—although there are some dogs who seem to like breakfast cereals. We find that liver is highly valued by most dogs. Cheese is another treat that dogs seem to go all out for.

As owner and trainer, pick the treats based on your knowledge of what your dog likes. If what you are asking the dog to do is easy and low stress, you can use lower value treats. If you are teaching the dog something new or asking him to do something that is hard for him, you would do well to use a treat that is high value to the dog.

Punishment

Punishment means your pet experiences something unpleasant immediately after she does something you don't want her to do. It can be verbal, postural (using body language), physical, psychological or biological. Effective punishment makes it less likely that the behavior will occur again.

If you choose to use what I would consider active punishment (such as a swat or a collar correction), it must be delivered while your pet is engaged in the undesirable behavior—in other words, "caught in the act." If punishment is late, even seconds late, your pet may not figure out what behavior the punishment goes with. That causes frustration and fear in your dog. If your dog can't connect the punishment with a specific behavior, she may think you have gone crazy. Too much of this and your dog will be worried all the time about what you might do.

One Downside of Punishment - If the dog can directly connect an active punishment to you, it may erode your dog's trust. That's why punishment is most effective when it does not seem to come directly from you. For example, if you use a shake can, don't draw attention to the fact that the noise comes from you. Don't point the shake can at the dog and threaten.

Guilty looks - as interpreted by humans - are actually response postures. Animals may not have a human's sense of right and wrong, but they are good at figuring out that your presence, combined with a certain look, will likely lead to something unpleasant (punishment). Don't make the mistake of thinking this means the dog understands why you are upset. If your timing is not perfect, the dog may never figure out why you are upset. He just knows you are upset so he goes into an appeasement posture to say "please don't hurt me," because his only other options are to run from you or bite you.

Using physical punishment, such as holding the neck skin and shaking your dog or performing "alpha rolls" (forcing your dog onto her back and pinning her on the floor) can result in bites. When you do this, you force your dog into a corner—she must submit, struggle to get away, or bite you.

Many people assume that their dog will always choose to submit, but this is not so. If the dog chooses to fight and wins, you can be hurt and the problem has just been magnified.

Another issue with physical punishment is that it can be associated with the people who are present at the time the punishment occurs. For example, a pet who is punished for getting too close to a small child may become fearful of or aggressive toward children.

The Poker Chip Theory

I like the concept that author Jack Canfield called the "poker chip theory." Imagine that every time your response to your dog is positive, you are amassing "chips" with him. The more warmth, praise, and treats he receives from you as you train him, the bigger pile of chips you've built up in his eyes.

On the flip side, any time you have to make a decision that is unpleasant for him, it costs you some chips. When comparing the pros and cons of positive approaches versus unpleasant approaches, being positive is what accumulates chips. Accumulated chips provide a buffer for the inevitable uncomfortable decision. The chances of building a great relationship are higher when there are chips to cash in.

The Role of Fear

For me, fear is a very significant issue when dealing with a dog's life. Fear can come from improper socialization, from a dog's genetic background, or from learning events involving humans, other animals or the environment. Fear can make a dog's life miserable. When fear consumes a dog's life, everything is difficult for the dog. Many of the problems that require special help from a trainer or behavior consultant—even those that appear to be related to outward aggression—may stem from fear.

Knowing this, it is important that our plans to help the dog do not increase the dog's fear or anxiety. The plans must include reduction of fear. In some cases, dealing with fear and anxiety involves the use of supplements or medication. See Section 26.

Trauma History

If a puppy or dog has been exposed to a traumatic experience, such as being hit by a car, receiving rough treatment by another dog, being kicked, or being exposed to a very loud noise, that experience may make an indelible impression. Overcoming it will require a specific approach and a big commitment from the dog's human partner.

Sometimes, a dysfunctional pattern of behavior in a puppy or dog derives from capricious use of punishment, such as a shock collar. For example, when a dog has no idea why he is being shocked, what is typically said by the user of the collar is, "The dog knows, or should know, why he is getting shocked."

Yet, in my experience, many people who use shock devices are not clear with their dog. The dog has not been trained to understand what is happening. To further complicate matters, the human involved is often influenced by how he feels at any given time. For example, if the owner has a bad day, the dog may get shocked for things that he would not get shocked for if the owner was having a good day.

Another example might be the dog who runs away and, when she returns, gets a beating. Consider that... "I come back, you beat me, and I'm supposed to want to come back."

Or how about a dog who is on a "Down" cue when a child intentionally jumps on the dog's front legs. What do you think that dog's perception of kids might be? Traumatic experiences like these can become a strong influence in that dog's life, and we must incorporate a plan of training to help mitigate this damage.

Overprotection

I address this as a separate category because it occurs so often. When a dog seemingly wants to be with his owner at every moment, clings and whines when he's not getting attention, and is always rubbing against or pushing on his owner, the dog may be the product of overprotection. This overprotection can be reinforced by the owner who believes the dog loves him so much that he can't stand to be away from him. This is so good for the human ego that it can be hard to consider it is not good for the dog; it is actually spawning a dysfunctional relationship.

When done while the dog is a very young puppy, it can be the basis for lack of socialization, which makes development of a balanced relationship more difficult. For best results, follow the guidelines in the socialization program earlier in this book, or develop and follow a program designed jointly by you and your behavior consultant. Either way, make sure you are only reinforcing behaviors you want.

Section 14: Communicating with Dogs

People have interesting beliefs about the relationship between dogs and humans. For some, the relationship can be summed up as, "The dog should do what I say because I say so." For others, it means bringing the dog up as you would a child. For still others, their dog is to be babied. When asked what's in it for the dog, befuddlement often hits. It's as if that part of the equation has never been considered.

The Communication Gap

That's when I suggest that many of the issues between dogs and humans exist because **people tend to treat dogs like humans in furry suits.** They act as if the dog comes equipped to understand English and can follow complicated phrases and lectures about behavior. On top of that, some people believe that dogs should have the same value system as humans. Dogs should know that your carpet is valuable and your couch is new and should not be marred.

While the human is treating the dog as a human in a furry suit, the dog is looking back through dog eyes hoping the human will communicate as a dog might. All in all, an irresolvable dilemma—unless the human decides to step up and figure out how to **close the built-in communication gap that exists because we are two different species.**

To close this gap requires a clear structure created by the human for the dog. It means simple, clear, consistent cues and behavior markers used all day, every day. This is easy for humans to intellectualize, but not so easy to implement. Almost every dog owner I have met acknowledges the issue when it is presented. Each nods in agreement. And yet, when communicating with their dogs, most continue to act as if they are humans in furry suits. This is a habit, and to break a habit requires commitment from the human partner.

Formal and Informal Life

There is a difference between good manners and formal obedience. Both are important and both can be taught. A dog with good manners knows how to conduct his or her self in most social situations. A dog with good manners will need to spend less time in formal, non-negotiable obedience positions. Good manners can be taught with consistent application of behavior principles and a clear structure.

We are teaching our dogs all the time. It's important that we are clear about our expectations so we can reinforce them. Take time to get a clear idea of what you want from your dog. If you can't state your expectations, they are probably not clear in your mind. If you are not clear, you will never be able to communicate your desires to your dog.

Good Manners and Simple Cues

My personal definition of good manners is standing, walking, sitting and lying down, with no vocalizing (unless that's part of a specific strategy). That means 24 hours a day, seven days a week, we must pay attention to our dog's behavior and let him know what behavior we like and what we don't want. For me, this involves setting up two specific cues and using two different voice tones to mark behaviors.

These cues are:

- **"No"** (said in a normal, not screaming, not intimidating voice) is used to mark behaviors that I do not want. I want the dog to learn to interpret the sound of "No" as simply "that's not what I want" (not as a threat of any kind)

- **"Good Boy"** or **"Good Girl"** (said in a different tone - happy, lovingly soft. or Smurf-like if you can identify) is used to mark behaviors I like. I want the dog to learn to interpret this sound as "you are doing the right thing and I like it."

In our informal life, we don't impose too much on the dog except the expectation of good manners. If the dog volunteers to lie down beside me I tell her "Good Girl" (as in, "good choice") and she is not required to stay in that position because I did not cue it (ask for it). Likewise, if my dog sits beside me voluntarily, she is not obligated to remain in a sit position. She can get up and move away any time she wants as long as she maintains good manners.

In our formal life, things are different. When we formally ask the dog to do something ("cue her"), we want to have established that the dog understands she should do what the cue requests, and remain in the position requested until she is formally released.

Formal and informal context are very important. In the informal, the dog manages her own behavior, is acknowledged for the things we like, and no formal cues or releases are involved. **In the formal context, the dog does as cued and remains as cued until officially released**. Keeping these distinctions clear makes life and communication with your dog much easier.

Bear in mind that "good manners" are a human idea. Dogs left to their own devices would not come up with these strategies as a way to impress humans in social situations. Therefore, we need to work, not only on our relationship, but also on our *specific communications with the animal*. Being clear and consistent in our training and feedback are what educate the dog.

Choosing Cues

If you don't like my choice of words for those two types of feedback, pick your own. You could just as easily say "Goldfish" where I say "No", or "Gosh" where I say "Good Boy" or "Good Girl." Our dogs don't come equipped with knowledge of English or any other language common to humans. It is our job to teach the dog what a given sound (which we call a *word*) actually means. So again, you pick the sound and teach your dog to associate that sound with something - a physical behavior, an item, a place. My only cautions are to be consistent, and don't get so fancy that you might forget the cue under pressure.

I once watched a handler work her dog in an obedience competition using only baseball terms. She used "batter up, home run, first base, second base, etc.," and the dog worked beautifully—I think maybe even to the tune of a first place in her division. You may also have heard of police or military dog handlers using a foreign language to cue their dogs. This may make it harder for others to influence the dog, because he doesn't respond to typical English words.

Consistency

By using uniform cues consistently, you give your dog feedback that helps him understand what you, as a human, want and don't want. Remember, you must teach your dog these things and make it worth his while to learn them. As a dog, he doesn't care about many things that are important to humans. He would actually prefer that we respond or react to him as another dog would react.

What's In It for the Dog?

I frequently hear people say, "I call my dog and she just looks at me like I don't exist." When I ask why the dog should come when called, some answer, almost in surprise, "Because I said so." As if response to a human directive is genetically built into the dog. Guess again.

Why should she stop what she is doing just because someone said "Come here"? The dog may be thinking, "Don't they know that there is a strong scent of a field mouse right here in the yard? Don't they know that my territory has been invaded by someone from outside?"

Realize that the dog has her own autonomy. She has an independence about her. We humans are only part of her life. We have some relationship with her and we have the opportunity to have a very significant and powerful relationship... but it takes some effort on our part. We have got to consider what's in it for the dog, if she is to see us as better than the scent of a rabbit.

What this means, in most cases, is either we work with the dog from a traditional training sense, where the dog chooses to do what we ask in order to avoid being Punished. or we work with the dog in such a way that she chooses to do what we ask because she gets something she likes in return.

The choice comes down to - what kind of relationship do you want with your dog? Do you want it to be based on punishment and intimidation or do you want it to be based on mutual enjoyment?

For me, it seems there has been some higher power involved in bringing dogs and humans together. I often wonder why dogs would want to be as close to us as they do. Even though we are supposed to be the more highly evolved of the two species, the treatment that some humans give dogs is often horrendous. They offer us the opportunity for great relationships and we respond with selfishness. We tie them to a post, exposed to sun and rain. We forget to fill their water dish. We let their coat get matted and covered with burrs. And when we call, we expect them to come because it's us. Wow!

Section 15:
Training 101 - Symbolic Feeding

Leadership and Bonding

Leadership and bonding involve some symbolic processes. Some trainers don't subscribe to the value of the type of symbolic activities I suggest, but I use them because the concepts have worked in the vast majority of settings where I have suggested them.

As a caution, remember that children are the least likely to be accepted by dogs as ranking members of a family group and, therefore, should not be the ones to initiate this protocol. The only obedience cue the dog has to follow, as we begin, is "Sit." (Much more on specific cues in the next section)

The idea here is to use a normal feeding process to provide a structure that keeps your dog healthy and helps her understand her place in your family.

First, a plug for condition-based feeding. This means you control the amount of food your dog gets based on her needs, not necessarily her wants. Like humans, some dogs will eat to excess unless a structure exists to help monitor what is actually needed. If you have questions read about Dog Food in Section 6.

The Step-by-Step Feeding Procedure

Now to the process. Determine how many times per day you

are going to feed your dog. Under normal circumstances, one or two times per day is fine. If your dog has special needs, or for puppies, more feedings may be appropriate. If you believe your dog may have special needs, talk with your veterinarian to get the best advice.

Once you have determined the number of times you will feed your dog, I suggest the following feeding protocol.

- Put your dog's bowl on a bench or table so he can see you prepare the food and place it in the bowl. This is a symbolic way to show you are the provider. If your dog lived on his own, he would spend most of the day searching for enough food to survive. He would understand that food is valuable and scarce. This ceremony makes a visual connection with you as provider of this valuable commodity every time the dog has access to food.

- Next, have out on your preparation table something symbolic that you can eat. It can be a vitamin pill, a jelly bean, two peanuts, a small glass of juice... it doesn't matter; it's symbolic. This is not about eating a meal before your dog eats. It's about stopping for a second after you fill your dog's bowl and eating your symbolic treat, then going on with the process. This action says to your dog that you have status, you make decisions. You don't have to do this part of the process every time you feed the dog. Do it more in the beginning of your relationship and then less often.

- Third on your protocol is to pick up the dog's dish from the table or bench, hold it about shoulder height and ask your dog to do something. The dog must show cooperation in order to get his food. This usually means something simple like "Sit" (assuming your dog knows what that cue means. If not, learn about the "Sit" cue in the Section 16– Fundamental Cues).

- Cue your dog to sit. Watch for your dog's rear end to hit the ground. This is the achievement of the "Sit" cue. As the rear hits the ground, say "Good Boy," as in "you did the right thing and I like it." Then immediately release the dog with your release cue (I use "Okay")—and put the food down for the dog to eat.

Here is the way it looks and sounds:

- "Sit" (watch for rear to hit the ground)
- "Good Boy" (you did the right thing),
- "Okay" (you are free to get up from your sit)
- Put food down immediately.

- Leave the food down for a predetermined length of time— 15, 20 or 30 minutes. At the end of this time period, if the dog has walked away and left food in the bowl, pick up the bowl and all traces of food and put it away until the next scheduled feeding time.

If, at the end of that time, the dog is still in the process of eating, he is allowed to continue until he has finished or has walked away from the bowl.

Some will ask, "But what if my dog doesn't eat? Shouldn't I give him another chance or leave the food down longer?" Not unless your veterinarian has determined that your dog has special needs. Otherwise, your dog will soon adapt to the schedule. Don't weaken.

Many clients find this concept easier to accept when I explain that they would never think of putting a meal on the table and then allowing their children to come back and forth between eating, coloring, and watching TV or playing with toys. Meals are offered at a specific time and require certain polite manners.

"But what if my dog won't sit?" Stay calm and committed to the process. Do not repeat the cue. You are holding the all-important card... *his food*. Wait as long as you can stand it. When you can't stand it any longer, say, in a normal conversational tone, the word "No" (that's not what I want) and then repeat the cue "Sit."

Again, wait as long as you can stand it. Repeat this process up to three or four times. If your dog knows the cue and does not respond, put the food away until the next scheduled feeding time and repeat the process. The dog will get it.

Then Up the Ante

Continue the feeding protocol for four or five days, until you and the dog are comfortable. Then you up the ante. That means you are going to require more from the dog in order to get his food.

- Do the same symbolic preparation activities as before. Cue "Sit," and wait for the rear end to hit the ground. Say "Good Boy," **then lower the food bowl about 10 inches *without* saying "Okay."** This means the dog has not been released. If the dog holds the sit as you lower the bowl those 10 inches or so, say, "Good Boy," then "Okay" and put the food down.

- If the dog moves while you are lowering the bowl (before you stop the bowl and release with "Okay"), say "No" (that's not what I want) and lift the bowl back up to shoulder height. Cue the "Sit," acknowledge with "Good Boy" and then lower the bowl again. If the dog holds still as you lower the bowl those 10 inches, put the bowl down, say "Good Boy," use "Okay" for the release, and let the dog come forward to eat.

- If the dog moves on the second, third or 10th attempt, calmly say "No" (in a conversational tone), move the bowl back to shoulder height, cue "Sit," acknowledge with "Good Boy," and repeat the process. After this has been successfully mastered, repeat this step for five days or until the dog has it down pat.

- The next step is to do all the preliminaries and then lower the bowl from shoulder height down an arm's length. Repeat the same process as in the previous step. Do this part of the process until your dog's performance is reliable.

- The final step includes all the preliminaries and you lower the bowl all the way to the floor. Watch closely as you do this. The dog is more likely to break your "Sit" cue as the food gets closer to the floor. If he moves, say "No," move the food back up, cue "Sit," acknowledge "Good Boy," and lower the food to the floor again. When the dog holds the sit until the food is on the floor, release him to eat with "Okay."

Remember, you hold all the cards in this activity. There is no reason for you to give in. On average, it's best if your dog gets just enough food to meet his needs. That means there should not be food left over after his meal time. The amount stated on the food bag is just a guide. Keep in mind dog food is a lot like laundry detergent; the recommended amounts are just that and the manufacturer is anxious for you to purchase additional product. Your evaluation of your dog's physical condition should control the amount you feed. If you are not sure, discuss the situation with your veterinarian.

Summary

This protocol sets you up as a provider with status, all accomplished without any confrontation. You are in control of valuable resources the dog needs and wants. It helps teach the dog to cooperate to get what he wants. The dog learns that food is scarce and valuable. Finally, the dog does a formal obedience sequence every time he is fed - all without physical manipulation.

A similar process can be used for other "life rewards" as well, such as access to the outdoors. A dog who sits politely to be leashed and then released to cross a threshold is demonstrating polite behavior and those good manners are another way that a dog gives you what you want in order to get what he wants. If anything about this process concerns you, contact a professional for advice.

Section 16:
Fundamental Cues

Obedience training is usually thought of as mastering a series of commands that indicate what behavior we want the dog to do, combined with a release cue that tells the dog when he can stop doing what was requested. These typically include "Sit," "Down" and "Come." These cues enable the dog to work in a structured situation when required and are the crux of our "formal life" together.

The Cue and the Action

Remember, any cue you use is just a sound to the dog. It's not about English; it's about a specific sound that we and the dog come to associate with a behavior and a result. It doesn't matter what you use as long as you use it consistently. The dog can learn whatever behavior she can physically perform that you can connect with a specific sound and a pleasant outcome.

When teaching a cue, either verbal or with another signal, our goal is for the dog to complete the action - such as, to "sit" and maintain that position until she either hears a release cue (such as "Okay" said in an upbeat tone), or until she hears another cue she understands.

The Lure

Initially, you want to interest the dog in following a lure - in this case a treat - so that when we use a lure to teach a position the dog will easily understand and follow.

Orienting the dog to a lure is a simple process. For me, it means walking the dog around a room and periodically dropping a treat on the ground for the dog to find. At first, the treats are dropped in front of the dog's nose or right on top of the dog's head so she can't help but notice.

As the walk continues, I drop the treats so the dog sees the treat bounce but must search a little to find it. If the dog doesn't find the treat, I point to it and guide the dog. This process sets the dog up so she will follow a treat when it is used for a more deliberate activity, such as teaching.

"Sit" Position

Perhaps the easiest cue to teach is "Sit." The sound "Sit" usually means the dog puts his rear on the ground and stays there until you release him or give another cue that he understands.

Remember, even the simple "Sit" cue is only a sound to the dog. It only means something when the dog associates it with a particular movement. For this reason, it is not necessary to say the word "Sit" while you are teaching the dog to follow a lure into the sitting position. It is only **after** the dog will consistently follow the lure, having established muscle memory, that you start adding the "Sit" cue just before you start your luring motion.

After a few practice sessions, the dog will begin to associate the cue with the movement into the sit position. At that point, you can fade the lure.

Fading the Lure

Fading the lure means making it less obvious as you use the verbal cue. Make the lure motion less and less obvious each time you do it... shorten your arm stroke and make the presence of the treat less and less visible. Later, you may use the motion you made with the lure as the basis of a hand signal. Ultimately, you may want your dog to respond to a verbal cue, a hand signal or a combination of both.

The "Sit" cue is relatively easy to teach because the dog can easily be lured into the sit position. Take a delectable treat, hold it just above the dog's nose and move it toward the dog's tail. As you move the treat backward, the dog's rear end naturally goes down as the head follows the movement of the treat.

The instant the dog's rear hits the ground, you say "Good Boy," let the dog have the treat, and then quickly release the dog using "Okay" accompanied with your own quick body shift to the side to indicate for the dog to hop up. This quick sequence gets the dog in position, acknowledges he did it correctly, rewards him and gets him up with a release before he gets up on his own.

"Down" Position

When your dog can sit on cue, the next move is to teach the "Down" cue. We use the "Sit" as the platform for the "Down"... meaning, we start the dog in the sit position and move him to the down position.

One definition of "Down" (not used in formal competition) is simply to get the dog into a position with his belly on the ground. The dog can roll his hip into a relaxed position as long as he remains on the ground.

Our goal is to teach the dog that when he hears the sound "Down," he puts his body in a position with his belly on the ground. Further, we want to teach the dog that he remains in that position until he hears either his release cue or another cue he understands. (I'll explain why we don't use "Stay", in a moment.)

- Don't bother to say the word "Down" when you first begin. We want to first teach the dog to mechanically move into the down position. The mechanics of the down are simple. First, get the dog into a sit, either by asking for it with the cue or waiting until the dog sits. Remember, if you ask for the sit, you should acknowledge it with "Good Boy."

- Once the dog's rear end is on the ground, take a treat (I use a meatball-size lump of soft treat material) and put it under the dog's nose.

- As soon as the dog takes notice, start moving the treat clump slowly toward the ground. Go slow enough that the dog can follow, but fast enough that the dog can only sniff and lick.

- As the dog follows the treat clump into the down posture, reinforce with the sound "Good Girl." We use "Good Girl" as a reinforcer because the dog has become familiar with the sound as part of learning the "Sit" cue.

- When we can get the dog to follow our treat lure into the down position and we are sure the dog will continue to do so, then we start adding the "Down" cue just before the lure motion so the dog can associate the cue and the mechanical motion of going into the down position.

- Once the treat reaches the floor, slowly move it outward along the floor and away from the dog's nose. Again, go slowly enough that the dogs stays interested. The dog should slowly walk herself into the down position. If the dog lifts her rear end off the floor as she follows the treat, quickly say the word "No" (as in "that's not what I want") in a conversational tone and move the treat away from the dog. Have the dog sit and begin again. Remain calm; if you are frustrated, the dog will pick up on this and become anxious. This will inhibit progress.

- Continue the process until the dog walks herself into the down position while following the treat. When the dog's belly touches the floor, say "Good Girl" and be sure the dog is getting some of the treat... actual bits or licks. Continue treating and saying "Good Girl" for a few seconds, then remove the treat as you say the "Okay" release cue and get the dog up with a quick movement of your body.

- If the dog does not follow the treat, you are either moving too fast or your treat is not of sufficient value to the dog to hold her interest. If she has just eaten a big meal or if there are distractions, it would take a very high-value treat to keep the dog's interest. If this is the case, take note and adjust the time and location of your training.

- If a dog doesn't follow your treat as you lower it below her nose and move it slowly away from her, try pushing the treat slowly in and between her front legs instead of pulling it away from her body. As you push the treat in, watch the way the dog hunches her body. Go with the direction she hunches. If the dog's body slumps to the left or right, use the treat to keep facilitating that movement down to the floor.

- Once the dog has learned the mechanical motion of getting into the down position, add the sound "Down" immediately before your treat lure motion, and you're on your way. Just remember, as you practice:

- Cue "Down"
- Acknowledge "Good Boy"
- Treat within two seconds
- Release with "Okay"
- Get the dog up

What About "Stay"?

You'll notice that I do not teach a "Stay" cue. Here is my rationale: Have you ever asked your dog to sit when you expected him to immediately stand back up?

When I ask that question, most people get a bewildered look on their face and, after a few confused seconds, say, "No." If that is true, and if "Stay" is to be a useful cue, you would have to say "Stay" immediately after using any stationary command. This means every time you cue a sit, it would require you to cue "Sit, Stay," even if you wanted the dog to sit for only a few seconds.

So if one cue will do, why complicate things by using two cues? Instead, **why not teach just one cue that means to assume the position and remain in the cued position until released by a clear release cue** (such as "Okay") or by another cue the dog understands (such as "Down")?

When they think about it, most of our clients conclude that "Stay" is not needed.

The Release Cue "Okay"

A clear release cue helps the dog to understand when he is finished, done, or off duty. I like the word "Okay" as a release cue. I say it with enthusiasm and something of a lilt in my voice. Some people don't like "Okay" as a cue because they believe it is too close to a conversational use of okay and that the dog may be confused and release accidentally when hearing the word used in general conversation. I have not had that experience, probably because I use body language and an identifiable voice tone along with my "Okay" release cue.

That being said, the release cue can be any sound that you can use smoothly and are comfortable with. Some other possibilities are "Free Dog" or "All Done." Remember, any sound can be connected with any behavior if you teach it that way. The word you choose is not important.

What is important is that without a clear release cue, your dog must try to figure out on his own when he is done. Is he released when you smile, say "Good Dog," move away, wave your arms? He must study you and hope he doesn't make a mistake. For the dog's sake, pick a clear release cue and use it consistently in all situations where you ask the dog to do something for you.

"Wait"

"Pause where you are until I say Okay" is how I use the cue "Wait." When my dog is about to exit my vehicle, I step in front of the door and say "Wait." After the dog settles down, I say "Okay," move away from the door, and let the dog out. I use the "Wait" cue any time I want a temporary pause. When necessary, I use my body to block movement as I say "Wait." After a while, my dogs pick up the meaning and the cue becomes easy.

"Good Girl, Good Boy"

As explained earlier, completing a cue successfully needs an acknowledgement - a clear sound that means "you did it" or "you did the right thing... and I like it." I like to use "Good Girl" or "Good Boy" as my acknowledgement/reinforcement sound. My goal is to say the sound immediately when the dog completes the cue. For example, if I cue a sit, I say "Good Boy" the instant I see the dog's rear end hit the ground. The rear hitting the ground is the culmination - the end result - of the position I asked for and I want to give that a clear acknowledgement signal.

Reinforcement

Reinforcement means doing something immediately after a behavior that increases the chances the behavior will be repeated. For example, if my dog sits and I give him a bit of food, my dog is more likely to sit when he is around me. If, every time he sits he gets a piece of cheese while no other behavior gets him anything he likes, sitting will become a big deal for the dog. He will likely volunteer to sit all over the place to get cheese.

Primary Reinforcers - Food, treats, water, going to potty, all these are primary reinforcers. That means you don't have to teach the dog to like them or want them. It's natural. The reason I use food as a reinforcer is because it's easy. Dogs like food. The only puzzle is to find out what treat the dog likes best and to use the treat when the dog is likely to be interested or hungry—like not right after a meal of roast beef.

Secondary Reinforcers - Something the dog is taught to like is a secondary reinforcer. The dog is usually taught to like the secondary reinforcer by having it paired (combined) with a primary reinforcer over time. A typical secondary reinforcer could be your voice saying "Good Boy." It becomes a secondary reinforcer by being combined with something the dog likes.

For example, when food is my primary reinforcer, and every time I say "Good Boy" I give the dog a piece of food within a few seconds, eventually my voice begins to be of interest to the dog. After the combination of "Good Boy" accompanied by a treat occurs over and over again, my use of "Good Boy" alone will serve as a reinforcer - something pleasant to the dog. Hence, my voice saying "Good Boy" is likely to encourage the behavior that came immediately before it.

Variable Reinforcement - If I give my dog cheese every time he sits, he is getting continuous reinforcement. If I give my dog cheese four times out of every five times he sits, he is getting intermittent or variable reinforcement. Sometimes he gets reinforced and sometimes he doesn't. It varies.

Usually, I recommend using continuous reinforcement when teaching a new behavior. Then, as the dog gets the behavior down pat, we switch to variable reinforcement. When we do this, we have to keep the dog guessing about when he will or will not get the reinforcer—often, a food treat.

Random Treating

A less technical way to refer to variable reinforcement is random treating. It's important to give the treat often enough that your dog will think it's worth it to keep working.

Not letting the dog know when he will or won't get a treat is also essential with random treating. To make it work, you must look exactly the same when you are going to give a treat as when you are not going to give a treat. If you somehow convey with your posture, how you hold your hands, the look on your face or the absence of a treat bag rattle, that no treat is coming, your dog will figure it out and may not perform when you cue him.

When we use random treating, we want our dogs to be like nickel slot machine players. People play nickel slots because they believe they have a high probability of winning. With nickel slots, you can keep playing without a high risk of loss and with a perceived good chance to win.

With our dogs, random treating means they win when they get the treat and do not experience much unpleasantness when they randomly don't get reinforced.

How many hits, rewards or getting the treat must the dog receive to keep him working? Not as many as you may think. I start with a treat for every repetition when I am teaching a new skill. As the dog learns or associates the cue sound and the behavior, I begin to reduce the number of treats. I do it in an organized way so I can tell if performance suffers. I might start with eight treats in my hand for a 10-repetition practice. I distribute the eight treats over the 10 repetitions in a random manner. If performance stays up, I may move to six or seven treats for 10 repetitions. I may continue this process until the dog can perform 20 repetitions with only one or two treat rewards.

If you are slowly lowering the number of treats and you reach a point where your dog's performance drops off, be sure you are not inadvertently revealing treat versus no treat. If that is not the problem, up the treats to a frequency that brings his performance back. Then slowly move to reduce the treats again.

Your Part

It's not just the treat rewards that reinforce the dog's performance. It is your personal reaction. Do you get excited at the right time? Do you use your voice and body to generate enthusiasm? Do you manage your voice and your body so that they work in your favor?

Everything you do influences your dog's reaction. Some things are enjoyable for your dog, some things are neutral and others make the dog uncomfortable. You must become a good enough reader of your dog's body language to know how you are affecting him. You need to be aware that if you touch him he might not be able to focus, and if you get too excited he can't concentrate. You learn this by paying attention to your dog's reactions. Finally, when cuing your dog, you can't disclose what reward he will get...or not get.

When training your dog, if as you give your dog a cue he hears you reach into your treat bag and rattle around for a treat, he knows what's coming. Likewise, if you cue him and he hears no rattle of the treat bag, he knows what's not coming. Even more obvious is if you wear a treat bag when doing formal training and not when out on a walk, the dog definitely knows the difference. This can affect performance. The game for you is not to give yourself away.

Notice how you hold your body. Where are your hands? Are you conveying things to your dog that are not included in your cue? Generate the same enthusiasm and body energy whether you are giving a treat or not. That will affect the dog's performance. He will be a more consistent nickel slot player.

Generalizing the Cue to Work Anywhere

Generalizing a cue means the dog understands that "Sit" means the same thing no matter where or when you give the cue. To achieve that, you'll need to practice the cue in a variety of situations so he will learn that no matter where he is cued, it always has the same meaning. By doing this, you avoid having to say to your dog trainer, "He always does it at home so I don't know why he won't do it here."

Practice cues in 10-minute sessions. Start in the quietest room in your home. Practice both sits and downs. Move the dog each time you give the cue. The sequence should be: "Sit," "Good Boy," treat, "Okay," move to a different location in the room. Next, you might do a "Down," "Good Boy," treat, "Okay," move to a different location in the room. Next you might choose to do "Sit," "Good Boy," "Down," "Good Boy," treat, "Okay," and move to a different location in the room.

After you have worked all around the quiet room, move to a different room and then a different room. Each time you practice, move to a room with more distractions. After you have practiced in all the rooms in your house, try the basement, the garage, the driveway, the yard, the sidewalk, then the local park. Then be creative. The more places you practice with your dog, the better he will understand that the cue always means the same thing, no matter where he is or what else is going on.

For the first 20 to 50 times you practice the cue, be sure to use "Good Boy" followed by the treat. This helps implant the cue in the dog's mind and it also helps establish your voice saying "Good-Boy" as a secondary reinforcer. After 50 to 100 repetitions with the food treat, you can move to random treats following your "Good Boy."

Duration and Distraction

Keep in mind we have encouraged you to teach your dog

gradually, incrementally increasing the criteria you expect. It is always important not to try to go too far, too fast. A famous animal trainer, Bob Bailey, reminds us to "Split, not lump." I like to think of this in terms of how cartoons were originally made. Drawings were made and then shown in rapid succession, every frame was a small slice in the progressive "picture."

The client is encouraged as they work on these beginning cues to think first in terms of duration. The cue is given (i.e. "sit") which is the beginning. The dog offers the cued behavior and as his bottom hits the ground, the handler says, "Good boy" and delivers a treat to reinforce that behavior. To signify to the dog the "end" of the behavior, the handler gives the release word "okay", then moves his body to signal the dog that he can move as well. The exercises are brief at first, then the client may start lengthening the amount of time the dog keeps its bottom on the ground. This is done by watching the clock; as the dog gets more reliable the time is gradually extended. This is establishing duration.

Trying to also add distance and distractions at this point, is probably going to be too much for the dog. Of course, there are always going to be some distractions in the environment but we also do our best to set the dog up for success by initially choosing environments that offer low level distractions. As the dog's duration improves we can then start to add distance and/or distractions, starting with a shorter distance and adding greater length as we progress. Distractions are made more difficult over time, and as the dog increases his reliability.

Distance

How close the dog is to you may determine how well he pays attention. I assume you are following my suggestions for creating structure and dealing with inappropriate behavior. I also assume you are using positive reinforcement rather than punishment when training. If so, you're likely to find that the closer your dog is to you, the better your control will be—at least in the beginning.

To continue, teach your dog to do cued positions close to you. Don't be in a big hurry to see how far away you can get from your dog until he is rock solid on cues. Proof him by staying close, moving around him, even sitting down and standing up to see if he holds the cue. Next, in gradual increments, have adults, kids and other safe dogs walk past him as he holds the cue.

When he can handle distractions like these, cue the dog into position and start moving away from him in small increments. Invent distractions, test your dog. As he becomes solid at four feet away, add another foot. Keep testing. When you reach a distance the dog can't handle, go back to a distance where he is solid and spend some more time before adding more distance.

With this approach, you are in a position to reinforce your dog for good performance rather than constantly having to replace or correct him for moving before the release. We'll look at Duration in more detail in Section 21.

Section 17:
Safety, Responsibility and Liability

As a dog owner, you are always responsible for preventing unwanted situations, managing those that happen by surprise (not because you failed to think ahead), and providing training so that your dog can function safely in a human world. If you don't do these things, your dog's life is at stake—either because of a mistake that appears to be aggression, or a mistake that ends up with the dog running away to be caught in a trap, killed on the road, or shot by a disgruntled human.

In addition to your responsibility for your dog's life, you are at considerable risk from a liability standpoint. If your dog harms another or destroys property, it can cost you big money. If you are insured, it can cause cancellation of your insurance.

Thinking Ahead and Planning

The dog owner is responsible for the environment where the dog lives, trains, and visits. In today's world, dogs cannot understand or anticipate all of the factors that may be dangerous to them or in which they are dangerous to others.

When the dog is young, immature and not fully trained, it's important to think ahead and use prevention and management. Don't wait until an undesirable situation occurs; you are in trouble at that point.

In short, dog owners need to be creative planners. Dogs need guidance in a human world. Humans must provide that leadership. It can't be left to chance or a lackadaisical approach. For dogs and humans to have a good relationship, the human must consider it important enough to think about and plan for.

If you pay attention to your dog's behavior, you can become able to predict unwanted behaviors and the situations that trigger them. Your job is to be creative and come up with ways to prevent those trigger situations.

Case Example: Welcoming Guests

When guests come to your house, does your dog jump on them? If so, and if you know this in advance, are you planning a way to prevent the unwanted behavior? If not, you are allowing the behavior to become stronger with each rehearsal.

Creative planning in this case could be as simple as putting your dog on a house leash before welcoming your guests. This strategy may not be the ultimate solution to the problem, but it may be the perfect solution early in the process.

Case Example: Stealing Food

Does your dog counter surf? Steal food? Stick her head in the kitchen trash? Do you know ahead of time that this is likely to happen? If you do, you are creative enough to find preventive solutions that are either permanent or for short-term use while a better training solution is being designed.

Being Around Other Dogs

For your dog, everything she experiences is part of her environment. Everything! That includes other dogs and their handlers. Any movement of another dog may be noticed by your dog, especially if she is continually scanning (checking out movement).

Whether you are taking a walk or attending a training session, other dogs become part of the environment that affects your dog, and it can change quickly. Other times a dog is so much a part of the environment that we can become desensitized to his presence - resulting in our lack of attentiveness. At this point, all it takes is an eye lock or a bump and the result can be very uncomfortable for all.

Many dogs don't have the skills to meet another dog without causing a reaction, so the owner's responsibility is great. If you add to all this the belief of some humans that all dogs should get along, the problem is magnified even more.

This means that **you as a dog owner must take personal responsibility to manage your dog so that she does not get hurt and does not cause harm to another**. Always know what is going on in the environment, even at your training school. Think ahead. Move your dog to areas that you can control. Condition your dog to focus on you when necessary.

Rehearsing Behavior - Prevention and management are important because **every time a dog completes a behavior, it is a rehearsal.** Every rehearsal makes the behavior stronger. We don't want our dogs to rehearse unwanted behaviors. This is enough reason to carefully think ahead about the situations we will take our dogs into. Consider what might happen, how your dog will react, and how you can plan carefully to prevent behaviors you don't want.

Caution About Dogs off Leash

A key component of safety for you and your dog will be their training on leash, which we will cover in the next section. I sometimes hear statements like these from clients:

"My goal is for my dog to come when called when he is off leash."

"I want my dog to stay in my yard without a leash or fence."

Each time I am presented with goals of this type, I respond by saying that I am extremely conservative when it comes to the safety of my dogs. Because of the way the world is today, I choose not to let my dogs off the leash unless I am sure I am in a secure area. Although I have several dogs who might be considered 95% reliable off leash, it is the other 5% of the time that can be the cause of their death.

It's during that other 5% that they see the squirrel, rabbit or bird and decide to pursue. As an example of the devastation that can occur when this happens, here is the text of an email received on an e-list we moderate.

"Yesterday, my dog was hit by a car and killed. It's my fault. I let go of the leash for a split second to shut the door. He was lying down on the porch enjoying a bone. He leaped up and ran out into the street. It's entirely my fault. I can't live with the guilt and the pain. It hurts too much just to force myself to breathe from minute to minute.

He was the center of my life and my greatest love. I have no coping mechanisms to deal with this loss, so I don't expect to survive it, but I wanted to take this opportunity to warn everyone: NEVER, EVER LET GO OF THE LEASH FOR A SPLIT SECOND.

Every dog owner I talked to yesterday has taken a million tiny risks, made a million little bad decisions that haven't ended in avoidable tragedy. I never thought it could happen to me either. I worried obsessively about something happening to Dozer, but at the same time, it was surreal. I never believed, on some level, that it could happen.

Now my life will never be the same; I am permanently scarred and I don't know how I will get through today without him, let alone forever. He is gone and it is all my fault. Don't let it happen to your dogs."

Section 18:
Dogs on Leash

Leash Signals

Leash control is important to most of us because there are fewer and fewer places where it is safe to allow your dog to accompany you off leash. The leash is your signaling device to your dog. When your dog feels a change in the leash, it sends a message.

At first, a dog's reaction to leash pressure is clumsy. An uneducated dog bobs and weaves and runs out to the end of the leash. With your help, the dog learns that when she feels pressure coming from the leash, she must change what she is doing—slow down, change direction or back up.

A wonder dog (what I call dogs who have it all figured out) feels every nuance from the leash. You could hold the leash with one finger, do an abrupt change of direction and the wonder dog will follow with no noticeable leash pressure.

Inappropriate use of the leash confuses your dog. She should never feel pressure when she is doing what you want. If she is sitting or lying beside you, the leash should be loose. If she is walking beside you, the leash should be loose. If you keep the leash tight all the time, your dog does not get the chance to make a mistake and learn from it.

Every training procedure we give you is based on the premise that the dog's leash will be loose unless it is used to induce awkward pressure as a specific teaching strategy.

Puppies on Leash

When it comes to training, puppies are not much different than dogs. They respond to positive reinforcement. They learn if things are presented to them clearly. The only difference that may hold you back is their level of socialization or life experience.

If a puppy has never experienced a leash, it may scare him until he knows what it's about. To orient a puppy to a leash, put a short line on the puppy and let him drag it around the house and yard (while under your watchful eye, of course). When the presence of the line is no longer an issue for him, make it a little longer. Then pick up the end of the line and follow the puppy around with no pressure on the line.

Once the line is no threat, begin to allow the puppy to experience what it is like to find the end of his line. To do this, just let him walk out to the end of the line. When he gets to the end, don't allow him to walk any farther. Just hold the line. He may pull against the end of the line. No matter what, don't let him move forward while pulling against the leash.

You can coax him back, make kissing sounds, call his name, offer him treats and just be patient. Eventually, the dog will stop pulling and look back at you. When he does, call him, coax him, squawk like a duck—get him to come back to you without pulling him. When he comes to you, give him a treat and praise him.

To begin teaching him to walk on a leash, follow the instructions below.

Leash Walking

Walking a dog on leash can be a nightmare. It's most difficult for our older clients, for young children, and when the dog is an adolescent. Many people start the process by taking the dog for a walk. If things don't go well, they will add a walking aid. It might be a slip collar or a pinch collar. The assumption is that the collar is designed to teach the dog to walk correctly.

Usually the thinking is that if you put a slip collar on a dog, he will pull until the collar closes around his neck and then the choking will stop him from pulling. It doesn't work like that.

Unfortunately, taking a dog on a walk and teaching a dog to walk are two different things. It's like learning to read. You don't just hand your child a book and say, "Go to it." You start with learning letters, then sounds, then putting sounds together into words, then words into sentences, then paragraphs, then stories. Teaching a dog works the same way. We've got to teach the pieces and then put them together.

We start with one rule: **Never let the dog move forward while pulling.** If the dog gets to go forward while pulling, it's self-reinforcing.

From there you can find opinions galore. My approach is to start working with a flat collar to give the dog and owner some experience in attempting to walk without the dog pulling. If progress is not made, I move to power steering devices. My preferences include a walking harness, designed with the leash clip in front of the dog, on the chest by the breastplate. There are several companies that make these harnesses.

If the walking harness doesn't work, I move to a snout collar or a head halter. Again, there are several types on the market. I find most dogs more easily accept the harness. If the dog does a lot of head throwing, tossing his head from side to side, lunging and the like, the head halter provides more control.

No matter what device the leash is connected to, we still want the dog's handler to learn some walking technique. The crux of the technique is to teach the dog that when she feels pressure on her leash or line, she needs to back off or change what she is doing. This takes patience and practice. It can seem very tedious to the dog handler. **If you remember nothing else, you must refuse to allow any forward movement by pulling.**

This probably means planning your walks to be training sessions rather than your two-mile constitutional... at least until your dog gets in step. Heeling is not necessary in the early stages of training a dog to walk. Heeling is a more precise activity that may come later. My walks begin with a general cue, "Let's Go." This signals the dog that we are on a mission and that there are rules. My process is outlined below.

Equipment

You need a six foot leash or line long enough to allow a loose leash between human and dog. Where the leash hooks to the dog's collar, there should be a J shape as the leash drops down from the collar and then goes up to your hand.

Teaching the Leash Walk

Goal: The dog does not pull on leash.

Voice cue: "Let's Go" or "Come On"

Start your practice in a distraction-free environment. Orient the dog to the left side of the handler. The left side is the traditional dog walking side. If you are walking against traffic, you will be between the dog and the curb, keeping the dog out of harm's way of oncoming traffic.

- Visualize an imaginary circle at your left side with a line through the middle of it emanating from your outside pants seam. The front edge of the circle should be the farthest point forward for your dog's head where he can still pay attention to you. Your circle should be big enough that the dog can walk in it without his head being so far forward that he can't keep track of you.

- Starting with the dog positioned in that imaginary circle, say "Let's Go," "Come On," or a cue of your choice. Use this cue every time you go for a walk. Be consistent.

- Use treats to create a hot spot for the dog at your outside pants seam. When the dog stays at your pants seam, treat liberally.

- Watch the dog's head. In a short time, you will begin to notice where the dog's head goes in reference to your magic circle and when he is no longer interested in you and is beginning a walk on his own.

- At the precise instant when the dog's head is signaling that he is on his own (before he pulls the leash taut), **change directions**. Just go in the opposite direction. **Keep the leash loose** and signal your dog to come with you. You can use "Come On" or the kissing "smooch" sound. Encourage the dog to return to your side. When he does, treat, praise and keep walking.

- If your dog beats you - meaning you didn't respond quickly enough and he was able to run to the end of the leash - STOP immediately.• Hold the leash still. Wait the dog out; no forward movement.

- Eventually, the dog will get tired of pulling and not being able to go anywhere. He will turn his head and look back at you, creating momentary slack in the leash.

When he does, say "Good Boy," encourage the dog to move toward you as you walk off in a new direction. When the dog catches up to your side, praise and treat.

- Another option when the dog runs to the end of the leash is to gently and slowly move backwards. This will more quickly encourage the dog to turn his head toward you. When he does, encourage him. When he catches up to your pants seam, praise and treat.

- Repeat the process I have just described any time the dog loses track of you and moves ahead of you, eventually starting to pull.

- When you start walking in the real world, you may find that your dog walks nicely for part of the walk and tries to pull during another part. This allows you to use a flat neck collar for the easy part of the walk and then switch to the harness or head halter for the hard part.

- As the dog improves, try switching back and forth between the flat collar and the harness or halter, and pretending to switch back and forth, so the dog no longer pays attention to where the leash is hooked. When you can do that, your dog is getting it.

Section 19:
Neutral Behavior

An Important Alternative

I've talked extensively about reinforcing a dog's behavior by adding something he likes. And I've described the thinking that punishes a dog with something he doesn't like. But there is a third option - *Neutral Behavior* that gives the dog no feedback at all.

Unfortunately, it seems we prefer to love them or hit them. If you subscribe to the same value set that I do, you would not be in favor of hitting them. So in many cases, it seems like all you can do is love them, no matter what. But that isn't true! Neutral Behavior, also known as Ignoring Behavior, is a good tool to use with your dog.

Ignoring Behavior

Unfortunately, in the human world, neutral behavior isn't often considered. But neutral behavior gives the dog something to compare to positive or pleasurable behavior. This gives us the option of rewarding the dog when he does something we want, ignoring the dog when he is giving us something we don't want, and not having to punish him.

I know, the first question here is, "What do we do when the dog misbehaves?" The inclination for many is to punish. The problem with punishment, as explained earlier, is that it has a fairly big downside. My approach is to use prevention and creativity to manage situations so they do not become dangerous, and then ignore the dog when he offers behavior we don't want and that is not dangerous.

In this system, we reward the dog immediately when he gives what we ask for, and we act as if the dog doesn't exist when he doesn't. The ignoring is neutral behavior. You are now probably asking yourself, "How does ignoring or using neutral behavior cause the dog to behave better?"

Case Example: The Jumper

Let's say your dog is a jumper. He comes out of his crate in the morning and jumps all over you. Of course, he's just excited to see you. When you get home from work, he jumps all over you as he greets you. You know it's all because he is excited about seeing you. And it is also a great ego boost to have a dog who acts like you are the number-one person in the world. That is the very reason why ignoring or using neutral behavior (remember that means **no feedback at all**) can work to get behavior change.

The dog thinks you are the greatest thing going, the sun rises and sets on you. He may even consider you a god-like creature as he looks at you through his adoring dog eyes. Much of his life is focused on getting things he wants from you, including your attention and affection. Everything he does makes perfect sense to him, as a dog. Everything he has done (and continues doing) is being done because he gets something from it, and to date, his jumping hasn't failed to be fun for him, even though it is not fun for you.

Maybe you have yelled at him when he jumps. Maybe you

have kneed him, tried to grab his front paws, stepped on his toes or pushed him down or away. Yet he keeps coming back.

So what does that tell you? First, your plan isn't working! Maybe it isn't working because dogs are very tough. When we push or pull or hold them down, unless we get really nasty - nastier than most people are willing to get with their pet - the dog may see it as a game. It can be a very rough game and the dog may still be saying "bring it on."

If you doubt a dog's toughness or ability to play rough, just watch two large dogs play together. They body slam, pull each other down and roll around much more than would be comfortable for most humans.

So, what do you have to lose by trying neutral Ignoring Behavior? It gives the dog a taste of what it's like not to get something he wants from you, it takes away the need for you to confront your dog, and it teaches your dog that he gets what he wants by giving you what you want. Okay, so how do you do it?

How It Works

Whenever the dog jumps up, you calmly say the word "No," which means "that's not what I want," and then you symbolically go away. This is not intuitive, but you can learn to do it.

- It means you close up your body by folding your arms, you turn your head to the side (no need to turn all the way around), you close your eyes and you stand perfectly still, no matter what the dog does. **Your dog may be astounded.**

The first thought that probably goes through his head is, "This always worked before, so I guess I will have to try harder." You see, it makes no sense to your dog that you have stopped giving him attention (of any kind) for a behavior that has always seemed to work before.

- So he begins to work harder. He may jump higher, jump faster, run around you and jump, bark at you and jump, jump up and paw at you, anything he can think of that might get your attention back on him. **You must hold out.** No matter what your dog does to try to get you to pay attention by jumping, you ignore him. **No feedback**, only Ignoring Behavior.

- If you can hold out, one of three things will happen - a light will go on, he will get frustrated, or he will get tired.

- It does not matter which, because **at that moment**, the dog will stop the jumping... if only for a second and if only to look up at you, like it's *you* who doesn't know what you are doing.

- **At that second**, stop ignoring and say "Good Boy" (which means "you are doing the right thing and I like it") and pet the dog.

- As you do that, expect that the dog will immediately jump again. As soon as he does, you mark the behavior with "No" (that is not what I want from you) and do your Ignoring Behavior—fold your arms, turn your head to the side, close your eyes and don't move.

- Hold that position until the dog stops again. As soon as he stops, say "Good Boy" and pet him or give him a treat, or both.

- If he jumps, ignore; when he stops, make a rewarding fuss over him. Always mark the change with either "No" or "Good Boy."

- Be so consistent that the dog eventually realizes that when he lifts his feet to jump, he never gets anything. When he keeps his feet on the ground - sitting, lying down or standing, and not vocalizing - he gets all kinds of attention.

Always observe your dog's reaction to your behavior. When you say "Good Boy," how does your dog respond? Does he stay down when you say "Good Boy" and jump or become agitated when you pet or touch him? Be aware of these kinds of reactions and adjust your actions to get the behavior you want from your dog.

Ignoring, or consistently using neutral behavior when the dog gives behavior you don't want, will teach the dog how to know what you like, and that being ignored is not fun.

You can handle any non-dangerous behavior this way. If the dog whines at you to get attention, ignore him until he is quiet. If the dog barks at you to demand your attention, ignore him until he stops.

Seems dramatic, doesn't it? It is. The Ignoring Behavior, as explained here, is intended to be dramatic. That is because the dog is a better body language reader than we are. This dramatic approach sends a blunt, clear message.

After the dog becomes familiar with your use of the Ignoring Behavior, you will be able to simply say "No," shift your head slightly to the side, and the dog will know what you mean.

Self-discipline and consistency are the keys to success. If the dog annoys you by nipping at your pants leg, you can scream and fuss with the dog or you can maintain your "ignore" until the dog loses interest. The first will encourage the dog to keep going; the second will teach the dog to stop.

For some people, the thought of a dog nipping at their pants leg is a big deal. Others worry that if the dog jumps and they are wearing shorts, their leg could get scratched while they are doing the Ignoring Behavior.

The solution here is the ability to plan ahead. If you are watching your dog, you will be able to predict when he is likely to jump or nip. If you can prevent it, do that. If the situation doesn't accommodate prevention, prepare yourself. Until your dog is trained, wear appropriate clothes (not shorts) if you know the dog will jump on your leg.

Case Example: All Dressed Up

One of our clients who owns a Chesapeake Bay Retriever was used to being mugged every day when she came home from work. The excited dog would meet her and jump all over her. As it happened, the client was required to wear dress clothing to work. Our strategy for dealing with this situation was to have her take sweat pants and a heavy jacket with her to work. When she pulled into her driveway, she slipped the sweats and coat over her dress clothes before going into the house. The dog mugged, the client Ignored, the dog learned, and she now does not need the sweats and coat.

This may not be your choice for a solution, but you must admit it was creative and it worked. Another solution might have been to have her spouse put the dog in a crate 20 minutes before she got home and then let the dog out of the create after she was home for 20 minutes and the dog had settled down. Either might be effective.

Section 20: Attention and Recall

Confirm Your Foundation

From here, we up the ante. We have spent a few weeks working to establish a foundation structure and to build basic cues. Now we continue to expand the level of sophistication in your relationship with your dog.

Before you move forward, let's review what we have accomplished so far. We laid out a pre-training structure for life with your dog. We addressed some common questions asked by our clients. We introduced basic cues and symbolic feeding, and we gained success walking on leash.

Once you've learned these techniques and have been practicing them for about two weeks, 10 minutes per day for specific formal cues and 24/7 for in-home and informal structure, you should be ready to move on.

If you have not yet spent time working on the skills and structure outlined previously, please don't move on. You can read ahead; just don't start working with the new material until the previous material is locked in. I ask this because your dog will have an easier time and experience less stress if the foundation is firm.

If you were a client at our facility, I would ask you the following questions before we proceed.

Dogs As Family Members

- Are you successful in ignoring (giving zero feedback to the dog) when she offers undesirable behaviors that are not dangerous?

- Are you clear on who is part of your training program and who is not—meaning you must manage your dog in their presence?

- Is the dog solid on the symbolic feeding process? Does he sit and wait until released to get his food?

- Have you implemented the massage program? How is the dog doing?

- Do you have a clear position on what you expect from your dog in your home and with regard to getting on furniture and beds?

- Are you consistently using the sound "No" (in a firm but normal voice level) to mean "That's not what I want"?

- Are you consistently using the sound "Good Boy" (in a peppy happy tone) to mean "You're doing the right thing and I like it"?

- Does your dog know the "Sit" cue and immediately put his rear on the ground when cued?

- Does your dog know the "Down" cue and immediately put his belly on the ground when cued?

- Does your dog understand the release cue and know

that when he hears "Okay" he is free to move out of the position you previously cued?

- Have you generalized "Sit," "Down," "Okay," "No" and "Good Boy" to a variety of locations and situations?

If you are still having trouble with any of these areas, go back, reread the material about them and continue to work on them. Don't beat yourself up if things are not yet in place. It's simply a matter of how much time you have to devote to the process, and how difficult your dog is to work with. With consistent reinforcement, you will master this skill set. No one expects you to be a miracle worker. Even the fact that you are working through this at all, puts you in a very special group of pro-active dog owners.

When you can honestly answer "yes" to those questions, we can proceed to more advanced skills.

Attention Work

What I call *attention work* is getting the dog to focus on you - specifically, to look at your face on cue. Some people use cues such as "Look," "Look at Me," "Watch" or "Watch Me" for this.

As always, I prefer a less artificial cue... something that seems to fit more easily into my day-to-day life with my dogs...something I can use on the street without seeming odd or out of place. So my choice is to use the dog's name as a cue for attention.

The process for teaching the name as an attention cue involves three steps. All three steps are conducted with your dog on a six-foot leash while you are comfortably seated in your evening chair, perhaps reading or watching your favorite television show or video.

Step One: Charge-Up

With six delicious treats in your hand or in a dish at your side:

- Say your dog's name and stick a treat in your dog's mouth as you say "Good Girl" or "Good Boy."

- The dog does not have to do anything except hear her name, eat the treat and hear you say "Good Girl."

- Getting the treat does not depend on the dog's behavior; it's the charge-up phase.

- If your dog is watching Animal Planet on television, reach around and put the treat in the dog's mouth.

- The dog hears your voice say her name, then, within a second or so, she hears your voice say "Good Girl" and is receiving a treat. She is learning to associate her name with the treat.

- This helps the dog begin to become more attentive when she hears her name—especially when she hears it said by your voice.

- On the first day, move immediately to step two.

Step Two: Turn-Look

With six treats in hand and your dog on leash:

- Wait until the dog turns her head away from you. When her head is turned away, say the dog's name ONCE.

- When the dog turns toward you, say "Good Girl" and treat.

- When the dog again turns her head away, say her name ONCE.

- Wait until the dog turns and looks. Wait as long as it takes; if it takes half an hour, wait and say nothing.

- When the dog turns and looks, say "Good Girl" and treat.

- Repeat this process six times.

- On the first day, move immediately to step three.

Step Three: Final Focus

With six treats in your hand and the dog on leash:

- Wait until the dog turns her head *away* from looking at you, then say the dog's name ONCE.

- Wait until the dog turns toward you, then continue to

wait until the dog either looks directly at your face or gives a quick eye flick to your face.

- The hard part here is to be patient until the dog gets around to looking at your face. You are trying to "catch" this behavior when it occurs and then reward it. The dog may look around, focus on other parts of your body, look at the treat, fidget, sit, lie down, etc., until she finally hits on the behavior that you want: a look at your face or an eye flick to your face.

- If the dog goes after the treat in your hand, close your fist around the treat and ignore her. She needs to learn that she never gets the reward by going after it, only by giving you what you want.

- When the dog looks at your face (direct look or eye flick), say "Good Girl" and give a treat. Don't be stingy here. If you think you see an eye flick, say "Good Girl" and give the treat. After a few times, the dog will start to get the idea that it is the face look you want and the eye flick will move toward a face look.

- Repeat this process six times.

Do all three of the previous steps the first day you start working on attention. The second day, drop step one, do a couple of step twos to get started, then move to step three. After the second day, use only step three. I suggest practicing step three six times every day to strengthen the cue.

Practice attention work until the dog looks at you expectantly when you say his name. This "charges" your dog's name to your voice and gets his focus on you. When the dog does a quick focus on you at the sound of his name, increase the distractions.

Remember, **only say the dog's name once and use high-value treats.** If you add distractions and the dog doesn't respond, you have added too much too quickly. Go back to the level where you had success and move forward more gradually.

To increase length of time the dog will focus on your face, continue to say "Good Boy" and treat, then pause and say "Good Boy" and treat again. Continue to repeat this sequence and wait longer between each "Good Boy" and treat. If you would like to put a release on this cue, say "Okay" and interrupt the dog's focus by moving.

I also recommend you become aware of how you are using the dog's name. Since we make the name more significant with this process, **I suggest refraining from using the name unless it is significant**. Instead, use other terms of endearment in routine daily communications, such as "Honey, Beautiful, Handsome, Sweetheart or Buddy."

Recall

Recall means getting your dog to come back to you. Some people believe this should happen just because the human is the master and the dog is the dog. Many don't bother to think about what it is that would interest the dog in coming when he is called. For our discussion, I divide the recall into two categories: informal and formal.

Informal Recall

When you are hanging out with your dog in your backyard, at the park, at Grandma's house or even in your family room, and you call your dog saying, "Here girl, here buddy, come on sweetie," or the like, you are in what I think of as an *informal* recall situation. You have little control over the outcome. It's strictly up to the dog. She either comes or she doesn't; when she doesn't, it can be frustrating.

In the informal situation, your dog operates on her own motivational scale. I think of it as a 1 to 10 scale. You, as the owner or handler, are somewhere on that scale. Maybe you're an 8.5. If you're an 8.5 on your dog's scale and she is playing with a dandelion that is a 4.0, you win. The dog comes to you. If you call her and your Beagle is on the scent of a rabbit, which is a 9.5, you lose.

Your position on your dog's motivational scale can vary based on a variety of things. If you have been gone all day, you will be higher on the scale. If it's supper time for the dog and you call, you will be higher. If you've been with the dog all day, you may be lower. The bottom line is, the dog decides where you are on her scale, and her response reflects your position.

Formal Recall

The other approach to recall is what I think of as a *formal* recall. It is heavily structured and it involves developing a conditioned response in the dog.

Training relationship: To help make this work, I suggest that you first establish a solid training relationship with your dog. Symbolic leadership activities, a positively reinforced cue structure (including clear voice tones), and clearly understood behavior parameters are part of this relationship.

Formal recall cue: The formal recall cue should not be used for anything else. So, for example, if you use "Come" for your informal cue, don't use it as a formal recall cue. The formal recall cue needs to be clear, simple and comfortable for you to say. Some options include: "Come," "Here," "Now," or "Front." You can teach the dog to come using any cue you want. Just keep it simple.

Training Sequence: Formal Recall

- Start with your dog on a six-foot leash. Let the dog wander away from you to the end of the leash. If your dog won't leave you, have someone else walk him away from you a short distance with an additional leash, and then let go of that leash. Call the dog's name, followed by your formal recall cue (said distinctly). Then animate (cause excitement) as you move backwards away from the dog. The dog should chase you.

- As you move away, look for a spot where you can stop and the dog will end up landing in front of you in the sit position. Have a treat ready. Lure the dog to sit directly in front of you.

- The treats you use for the formal recall should be the best possible treats you can dream up. I often suggest this is the time to give your dog those bits of roast beef, chicken or cheese that you might otherwise withhold. In these exercises, always include a treat with your "Good Boy" as the dog hits the "Sit" in front of you. The randomness of treating in these exercises is what will the treat be, *not* whether there will *be* a treat. The idea here is for this cue to be perfect—so well-conditioned that the dog never considers anything else.

- Use the recall cue only once ("Spot, Come!"). Don't say "Sit" when the dog comes; instead, lure her into the sit position. Verbally praise the dog and give a high-value treat. Keep the dog sitting by using treats or a leash and collar if needed. Release her with "Okay."

- Practice until the dog will return to you, sit in front and remain sitting without the need for excessive body language or coaxing.

- Practice until the dog is proficient. My general rule is that the dog must be able to do nine of ten recall cues perfectly. He still must also do the tenth one, but it doesn't have to be perfect. It is not about how quickly you can get the dog off leash. The idea is that it does not even occur to the dog to skip or ignore the cue. Be 100% sure the dog will come to you. As the dog becomes reliable, add distractions.

- Once the dog is 100% reliable on a six-foot leash (that's a six foot distance away from you) with distractions, double the length of the leash by adding to it or use a long line. Repeat the process you used with the six-foot leash.

- Your energy level will make a difference in the dog's reaction. Use verbal and body language to encourage the dog to come to you. If the dog starts toward you, encourage with "good girl, good girl, good girl," or "pup, pup, pup," or "kiss, kiss, kiss" and the like. Don't repeat the dog's name or the cue.

- If the dog starts toward you, encourage her. If the dog moves away or gets distracted, jiggle the leash, like a pager vibration, and say "No, No, No," until the dog turns back toward you. Then, encourage again with high energy. When the dog does nine of ten perfect with ten completions, lengthen the line again.

Continue the process I've described and continue lengthening the line until you have the dog as far away as you want to work with her. Once you are 10 or 12 feet away, I like parachute cord for the long line, because it's light but is 500-pound test. Light cord is less intrusive for the dog. If you like a handle, tie the cord to the end of the leash and use the leash for a handle.

- Next, work the dog off line in your house. If the dog ignores the cue and runs away from you, put him back on line. Do not let the dog rehearse skipping your formal recall cue.

- You can also play hide and seek with your dog in your house. Go hide; use the dog's name and the recall cue and expect the dog to find you. When she does, wait for the "Sit," praise, treat and release. If high-value treats are used, the dog is less likely to break away.

Practice until the dog is proficient. If the dog is not proficient, go back to an earlier step, increase the treat value and lower the distraction level. Never let the dog rehearse behavior you do not want.

As for sitting in front of whoever gave the recall cue, the dog should be close enough that the handler can reach down and comfortably grab the dog's collar where she is sitting.

When your dog is off leash, call only if you think she will come. If you don't think your dog will come to you, don't call her; go get her. And remember, your dog will not come to you if she experiences unpleasant consequences for coming. If she is always put away, taken in or, heaven forbid, scolded or beaten when she finally does come, you are making the recall worse.

Once he is doing well off line in the house, you can take him outside in a safe area (fenced backyard) and begin calling him to you and playing hide and seek around the yard. Eventually you may want to call him from your house and give him his treat when he is sitting in front of you.

As to long distance recalls off-leash, *always be safe*. Use fenced areas (a football field, tennis courts, etc.) until your dog always responds perfectly.

Finally, if at any time your dog is not coming to you when cued, he probably does not understand the cue in that particular context. Go back a step and work with him further. **Do not let the dog rehearse unwanted behaviors.**

Section 21: Building Duration

If you were successful in working with the "Sit" and "Down," you should be ready to begin increasing cue reliability. By successful, I mean your dog now clearly understands what body position to offer when he hears the "Sit" or "Down" cues, no matter where the cue is given, and he knows that when he hears the sound "Okay," he can move out of the cue and relax... as long as he maintains good manners. If your dog doesn't yet have these cues down solidly, it can be frustrating for him to move forward.

Up until now, I have not suggested working away from your dog. I have asked you to practice using the "Sit," "Down" and release cues in all kinds of circumstances with you close at hand. This is a process of conditioning the dog to the cue sound. Now we will expand the dog's expertise.

The act of remaining in position until released requires a different kind of learning from that of putting the body in a specific position when one hears a particular cue sound or sees a nonverbal signal. Duration is an entirely different concept.

The Crossroads

We are now at a crossroads of sorts. Until now, we have suggested no activity that causes your dog even minor stress, unless you count stopping your dog from pulling and insisting that your dog sit to get her meals.

As we move into developing duration (in the "Sit" and "Down," cues which are well-mastered), I will present two possible scenarios: one for those who believe a dog should never experience any discomfort of any kind under any circumstances, and one for those who are willing to use what I describe as *awkwardness* to facilitate a faster learning curve.

Awkwardness

Awkwardness occurs when the dog tries to go beyond the length of her leash or tether. It results from pressure the dog exerts against some part of her body (via collar, harness or head halter) as she pushes against a line or tether.

Examples:

- **The dog forges ahead while on leash.** As she reaches the end of her leash, she creates pressure. The impact of that pressure depends on how fast the dog rushes to the end of her line. A good handler manages the situation so the dog has a limited space to move forward, therefore keeping the impact at the end of the leash soft. We are assuming that the owner is not jerking the dog as she runs to the end of her line. The handler just prevents the dog from moving forward once the end of the line is reached. The dog feels awkwardness as long as she continues to pull forward when the end of the line has been reached. As soon as the dog stops pulling, the pressure and the awkwardness go away. The handler then redirects, praises and rewards.

- **The dog is in a down position.** The handler has the ball of her foot on the dog's leash at a location that allows the dog full head and shoulder movement yet won't allow the dog to get into a full stand. The dog attempts to stand from the down position. The dog experiences awkwardness because he cannot stand all the way up. As long as the dog continues to put pressure on the leash by attempting to stand, the awkwardness continues. Once the dog returns to the down position, the awkwardness goes away.

If proper foundation work has been done so the dog understands his cue and has practiced and been reinforced, this kind of awkwardness is very low on the stress scale and very short-lived. If you don't find this to be true, go back and revisit your foundation work.

- **The dog is in a sit position.** The handler moves the leash so that it is directly above the head. The leash is loose and the dog has complete freedom of movement of head and shoulders. If the dog lifts his rear end off the floor, the handler applies *mild* pressure upward as the dog's rear lifts off the ground. Mild pressure is equivalent to that of a dress shirt and a tie on a human neck. For a dog, it's more an odd feeling than a stressful feeling. This awkwardness disappears as soon the dog's rear end starts back toward the ground. The pressure here is very mild—more a reminder to the dog that something is out of kilter. The dog can move around, even take a few steps with the awkwardness in place.

The key to this concept is that the awkwardness created by pressure the dog generates against a leash or tether is nothing more than a signal to the dog that something needs to change. The handler does everything possible to assist the dog in understanding what that something *is*. **There is no jerking in this process.** The right body language, the occasional lure, verbal encouragement—all these are used to communicate how to get rid of the awkwardness. These things, combined with good foundation work, make the process simple and low stress.

Awkwardness is not used with a dog who is not ready. It is the handler's responsibility to prepare the dog so that the awkwardness will not be a frustrating experience. At our facility, if a client has not done the required foundation work, we will not use awkwardness with the dog. We have no interest in frustrating the dog.

Duration in "Down" and "Sit"

Building duration in the down position begins with cueing the dog to lie down, as you have been practicing. Once the dog's belly hits the ground, acknowledge with "Good Girl" and treat. Keep treating while you make sure the dog's leash is laid out flat on the ground.

Now, put the ball of your foot on the leash at a point that does not put any pressure on the dog. Be sure the dog's head, neck and shoulders can move in all directions. If the dog is pinned or has pressure from the line, her learning is hampered. The spot where your foot is on the line should also fix the line to be short enough that the dog can't get into a full stand.

- So far, no awkwardness exists for the dog as long as she remains in the down position. Keep feeding the dog small treats while she is in the down position. When the dog and you are comfortable, stop feeding treats. At first, stay by your dog for a few minutes. If she stays down, praise and treat. Next, try standing up or move back a step from the dog. If the dog stays down, acknowledge with "Good Girl," treat, "Good Girl," treat, with varying intervals between each pairing of "Good Girl" and treat.

- Keep adding more time between sequences of "Good Girl" and treat. Eventually, when the interval between acknowledgment and treat is long enough or the right distraction occurs, the dog will attempt to get up. When she does, she will quickly feel an awkward pressure as the leash stops her progress. (Remember, your foot is on the leash.) When that happens, you say "No, Down" and wait. No leaning over the dog, no pushing on the dog, no stern voice, no pointing at the floor. Preferably no further talking at all; just let the dog process what is going on.

- If the dog immediately begins to struggle, something is wrong. Either your preparatory work is not yet done or there is another problem. If you think it's the prep work, immediately lure the dog back into the down position and release with "Okay," then go back and rework teaching the "Down" as described earlier, without the pressure.

If you think it is something else, it's time to get help from a trainer or a behavior professional.

- Many times, if you have practiced the work outlined earlier, the dog will calmly lie back down. If so, acknowledge and treat. Then move away or stand up and relax. If the dog stands again, repeat the same sequence. Be patient; allow the dog to learn without pressure from you. The awkwardness here is no different than that used to stop the dog when she runs to the end of the leash.

In general, in all processes, I want the dog to learn that when she feels a change in leash pressure, she should change what she is doing and look for a different behavior that alleviates the awkwardness. A correct change releases pressure on the line. The handler then acknowledges and reinforces the desired change.

- If, when the dog stands up, she begins to look as if she doesn't have a clue what is going on or she becomes agitated because of the awkwardness of the leash, show her your treat (put it under her nose) and then move it to the ground and tap the ground in front of her. Say nothing. Keep tapping the ground. She may nuzzle the treat. Keep tapping the ground and say nothing. She will lie back down. When she does, acknowledge and treat.

- If done correctly, the dog may experience what looks like a bit of bewilderment when she stands the first time and feels the awkwardness of the leash. As the dog processes what is going on - without your involvement - she may show the beginnings of a little frustration. Don't give in too quickly; let the dog process the information. When you think the dog has had enough time to think it through and yet has not laid back down, hold the treat to her nose and then move it down and tap the floor again.

- When the dog lies down, acknowledge and treat. Stand back up, periodically tell the dog "Good Girl," and every few "Good Girls," add a treat. Space the treats out farther and farther as the dog figures out the game. Be careful not to treat too quickly after the dog gets up and goes back down, because you don't want her to think it's a jump up, drop down game. She should get the treat when she has been in the down position at least a few seconds... long enough to know that it is the "Down" you are reinforcing.

From here, you should set goals for your dog. Start with a goal of 15 or 30 seconds. You want the dog to be a winner, so don't set goals she can't meet. Your experience with your dog should guide you to the appropriate length of time for a down. When the dog reaches the 15 or 30-second goal, release her with "Okay" and make a fuss. Once that first goal is easy, add another 15 seconds. When she gets that one, add another 15 seconds. When you get to a minute, you can probably add 30-second increments. After the dog gets to three to five minutes, you may be able to add one-minute increments.

The important thing is that the dog wins every time. If she is fighting with you about staying down, your foundation work is not yet in place, you're trying to progress too fast, or there are too many distractions.

Your dog *will* get this. Relax; it's about getting it done, not how fast you get it done. You want to accomplish the task and you also want to keep your relationship intact. When your dog starts accomplishing your goals, the sky is really the limit. You can keep adding to the goal until your dog can hold a 30- to 60-minute down if you wish.

One thing I ask is that you don't get into the "let's see how long we can keep her down" thing. When you do that, the dog has to lose because the only way you know how long she can stay down is to wait until she gets up. I'd prefer that you set goals you know are attainable. If you keep your focus on your dog as you go along, you will have a good sense of what your dog can do and how fast she can progress.

After a while, if the dog forgets and starts to get up, the awkwardness of the leash will be a quick reminder to the dog. He will immediately return to the down position as soon as he feels the slightest sensation from the leash.

We have noticed that the down is the easiest position for both dog and handler to get an understanding of duration when using this approach. After about a week, with daily practice, the dog seems to get a handle on how awkwardness relates to duration. After about a week of working on the down position using this procedure, it can be applied to the sit position and the dog will get it quickly.

Steps for the sit position follow. They are similar to those for the down.

Building duration in the sit position begins with cueing the dog to "Sit" as you have been practicing. When the dog's rear end hits the ground, acknowledge with "Good Boy" and treat. Keep treating while you arrange the leash so it goes up directly above the dog's head to your hand. Be sure the dog's head, neck and shoulders can move in all directions. If the dog has pressure from the leash, his learning is hampered.

- So far, no awkwardness exists for the dog as long as he remains in the sit position. Keep feeding the dog small treats while he remains in the sit position. When the dog and you are comfortable, stop offering treats. Stay by your dog. If he remains in the sit position, praise and treat.

- Next, try moving one step away from the dog. If he remains sitting, acknowledge with "Good Boy," and treat. Keep adding more time between sequences of "Good Boy" and the treat. Eventually, when the interval between acknowledgment and treat is long enough, or the right distraction occurs, the dog will get up. When he does, quickly and smoothly (no jerking) put light, awkward pressure straight up on the leash. At the same time, say "No, Sit" distinctly, and wait. No leaning over the dog, no pushing on the dog, no stern voice, no pointing. Preferably, no other talking. Just let the dog process what is going on.

- If the dog begins immediately to struggle, something is wrong. Either your preparatory work is not yet done or there is another problem. If you think it's the prep work, lure the dog back into the sit position and release with "Okay," then go back and continue working on the cue without the leash pressure. If you think it is something other than the need for more practice, it's time to get help from a trainer or a behavior professional.

- Many times, if the training outlined earlier has been practiced, the dog will calmly sit. If so, acknowledge and treat. Then move away to a distance that is successful for the dog and relax. If the dog stands again, repeat the same sequence. Be patient; allow the dog to learn without pressure from you. In general, in all processes, I want the dog to learn that when he feels a change in leash pressure, he should change what he is doing and look for a different behavior that releases the awkwardness. A correct change releases pressure on the line. You then acknowledge and reinforce the desired change.

- If, when the dog stands up, he begins to look as if he doesn't have a clue what is going on or he becomes agitated because of the awkwardness of the leash, show him your treat, put it over his nose and then move it back toward his rear end. When he sits back down, acknowledge and treat.

- If the dog continues standing, be patient and use the treat and hand motion you originally used to teach "Sit." Don't give in too quickly; let the dog process what is going on. When you think the dog has had enough time to think it through, if he has not returned to the "Sit," put the treat to his nose and move your hand toward the rear end again.

- When the dog sits, acknowledge and treat. Periodically tell him "Good Boy," and every few times, add a treat. Space the treats out farther and farther as the dog figures out the game.

From here, you should set goals for your dog, as we did with duration in the "down." Start with a goal of 15 or 30 seconds. You want the dog to be a winner, so don't set goals he can't reach. Your experience with your dog should guide you to the appropriate length of time for a "Sit" goal. When the dog reaches the 15 or 30-second goal, release him with "Okay" and make a fuss. When that first goal is easy to reach, add another 15 seconds. When he gets that one, add another 15 seconds. When you get to a minute, you can probably add 30-second increments to your goal. A one or two-minute "Sit" is a good goal. If you want the dog in a stable position for longer than 2 minutes, use a "Down." It is easier for you and the dog.

- As I said before - The important thing is that the dog wins every time. If he is fighting with you about staying in the sit position, your foundation work is not yet in place, you're trying to progress too fast, or there are too many distractions. Your dog *will* get this. Relax; and remember, it's about getting it done, not how fast you get it done. You want to accomplish the task and you also want to keep your relationship intact.

After a while, even the slightest awkwardness will be a reminder to the dog and he will immediately return to the sit position—probably faster than you can say anything. Eventually, he will not even need the reminder.

If You Want No Awkwardness

For those who feel that the use of awkwardness as I've described is too much for your dog, you can accomplish the same end result using the same process but eliminating the use of the leash to provide awkwardness when the dog gets up.

Every time your dog gets up without being released, say "No," repeat the cue, and when they resume the correct position, reward. Use your "Good Girl," treat sequence to acknowledge the dog and reinforce. Keep realistic goals. If the dog is getting up frequently, your goals may be too much for her. Without the awkwardness, it may take you more time to build duration and your dog may be less reliable in maintaining the position until released. Keep working and keep your goals and distractions realistic.

The key here is *not to reward your dog for getting up*. This can happen if she gets up, you lure her back down and give her a treat immediately. If she does this repeatedly, she may think the game is "Stand up, lie down, get food." To curb this, be sure the dog is in a sit or down position for a few seconds before giving the treat. In other words, **make sure the dog knows the treat is coming for duration,** not for "Jump up, lie down."

Section 22:
Nonverbal Cues

Hand and Body Signals as Cues

Signals of any kind, used consistently and with clarity, can be used to let the dog know what we want. When a dog looks at us, she sees everything about us. What we must do is present ourselves in such a way that the dog can tell what she is supposed to pay attention to and what she can ignore or screen out.

A dog can pick up on a motion, even a small one, and learn that it signals an action. But dogs can have difficulty decoding the message we are trying to send if we are making too many movements or our movements are inconsistent. Our job is to decide what signals we want to use and make them clear and consistent.

Just about any signal will do, as long as the dog can pick it out. I have a friend who does all his nonverbal signals with his fingers. The movements are minimal yet very precise. His dog watches him like a hawk and performs perfectly.

Typical nonverbal signals involve movement of the arms and hands. They could be done with any part of your body that the dog can discriminate. My typical signals are:

- **"Come"**: An arm swing toward my chest, starting with my arm straight out to my side at shoulder height. My hand is open and at the end of the signal my palm ends up on my chest. The arm swing is motioning the dog toward me.

- **"Down"**: An arm swing down from the elbow starting with my arm bent 90 degrees and my hand at shoulder height. At the end of the signal my palm is open and facing the ground. The trick here is for the dog to see the palm of the hand moving downward. If the dog is 100 yards away, my arm movement may begin high above my head. If my dog is at my side, only the palm of my open hand with little movement may be enough.

- **"Sit"**: I begin with my elbow close to my body and my arm straight out in the front of my body. My arm swings up toward my chest. That's it.

None of my signals are magical. Don't worry if you have trouble deciphering my directions. Remember, any signal you invent and use clearly and consistently will work. You could bow your head for "Down," lift your left leg for "Sit" and bow at the waist for "Come," if that's what you like. Remember my friend who uses his fingers to signal.

Teaching Nonverbal Signals

When you use a lure to teach the "Sit," "Down," and "Recall," that motion can establish a foundation for nonverbal signals. Think back to when you used a treat to move the dog's head back so he put his rear on the floor or placed a food ball under the dog's nose to lure him to the ground.

Those motions may already be in the dog's mind. If so, those motions may help if your nonverbal signals are done with your arms and hands.

Even if you are starting from scratch, as long as your dog is responding reliably to your verbal "Sit," "Down" and "Come" cues, you can add a nonverbal cue. Here is how it's done:

- Perform your nonverbal signal and then immediately (within seconds) say your verbal cue.

- When the dog performs the cued action, acknowledge and reward. Release before the dog gets up on her own.

- Continue using this sequence until you notice your dog beginning to move into the cued position *before* the beginning of your verbal cue. Withhold your verbal cue a little longer after you give your nonverbal cue to test the dog's understanding.

- When the dog seems to understand the nonverbal cue, try using it without the verbal cue. If the dog performs the cued action, the non-verbal cue is in place.

- From that point, practice verbal cues only, nonverbal only, and both verbal and nonverbal together. If the dog's performance drops off, go back to the first step in this sequence and start again. The dog will regroup quickly. You can use a nonverbal cue for any action you can teach. The only criterion is that the dog must be able to see the cue. Always remember that you reinforce and release the action cued just as you do with a verbal cue.

Is the Clicker Quicker?

Karen Pryor has popularized the use of a clicker as a signal device. The clicker makes a noise like the cricket toy that some of us played with in the 1950s. It is usually about two inches long, an inch wide and one-half inch deep. There is a metal or plastic button that is pressed to get the click sound.

The click sound can be delivered very quickly to acknowledge behavior and it does not carry the emotion that may be in a human's voice or body language. As a signal to the dog, it's very efficient.

We use clickers when teaching certain complex behaviors that must be formed by connecting smaller pieces. We also use it with dogs who are so aggressive or so afraid that we can't get near them when we begin our work.

The clicker itself does not change behavior. It is only a vehicle for change. People can become very confused about this. One of our clients, fresh from an obedience class elsewhere, when she entered our facility, started clicking. When I asked about use of the clicker, she said, "I think it's supposed to calm the dog down." We had some retraining to do.

If you want more information about clicker use, visit Pryor's web site (www.clickertraining.com) and her book *Don't Shoot the Dog*.

Section 23: Establishing Home Base

Home Base

"Place," "Perch," "Bed," "Carpet," or whatever you want to call it, teaching your dog to find and stay with a portable station of some type is a good practice. This cue can be taught at any time during your foundation building.

I suggest using a small rug, mat, towel, carpet or other easy-to-clean material as home base—the "place" you send your dog. I like something washable. It also helps if the material lies flat without wrinkling. Your mat should be easy to carry. You can move it from room to room, to Grandma's house, or to the facility where you train the dog. No matter where it is, it provides a comfortable spot with a familiar scent for your dog.

Define the Goal

Teaching your dog to go to "Place" begins with a definition of the cue. "Place" can mean "go to your mat and lie down or sit." It can also have a more general meaning, such as "keep any appendage on the mat and you are in compliance." A tail or foot on the edge of the mat can qualify as contact. I have had dogs who will walk around the edge of the mat, lie down with one foot on the mat and never lose mat contact. You've got to define what behavior you want because that is what you are going to reinforce.

Suppose your definition will be go to the mat and keep some part of the body on it. With that definition to start, you will be reinforcing your dog when he hits the mat with any part of his body, often his foot.

Steps to Home Base

- Begin by getting your dog's attention and then throw the mat on the floor so your dog can see it.

- Show your dog a treat and use some body language pointing to the mat as you toss the treat on the mat. When the dog goes to the mat to get the treat, praise with "Good Boy." Continue dropping treats on the mat to keep the dog on it.

- Release with "Okay" and get him to get off the mat (before he just gets up to walk off of his own accord).

- Repeat tossing treats. Praise the dog when he steps on the mat, release and move him off the mat.

- When the dog easily follows the treat to the mat, add the cue "Place" or whatever cue you like. Say the cue just *before* you toss the treat onto the mat. Motion toward the mat, wait for the dog to step on the mat, then praise with "Good Boy," treat, release and move the dog off the mat.

- If the dog moves off the mat before he is released, say "No" (that's not what I want), guide the dog back onto the mat, praise with "Good Boy," treat, and when you are ready, release and move the dog off the mat.

- Initially, your release should be based on observing the dog. Use praise and reinforcement to encourage the dog to stay on the mat. When you have squeezed out as much time as you can get, release the dog and move him off the mat.

- Set goals as you did when developing duration for the "Sit" and "Down" cues.

- Be very consistent! When you ask, be sure your dog accomplishes the cue. Be sure you release him. If the dog moves off before your release, place the dog back on the mat, praise and reward.

- Repeat the previous steps from all angles of approach to the mat, then increase the distance from the mat.

- Finally, move the mat to different positions, rooms and geographic locations to generalize the cue and the "Place" action. If the process is not working, it's likely you are moving too fast or you are not being consistent. Go back and restart the process at a level where the dog can be successful. Ultimately, this process can be used as a home base for your dog for unlimited amounts of time at any location.

Section 24:
Time Out

Time Out

Everyone has their own idea about time out, what it is, how to use it, even if it should be used at all. Our experience has been that time out can be effective when used in a specific context.

What you will notice is that our approach to time out is very structured. If you just arbitrarily put the dog away when she does something you don't like, it's very confusing to the dog.

For time out to be effective, the dog must be able to connect a specific behavior with her time out. For example, it might be jumping on guests when they arrive at the door.

Here is the framework we use:

- With time out, work on changing just one behavior at a time. Decide what that behavior will be.

- Pick a cue to mark the behavior you are working to change. I prefer short, simple cues, such as "Too Bad," "That's It" or "It's Over."

- Every time the dog does the behavior, mark it once with the cue.

- Immediately after marking the behavior with the cue sound, take the dog unceremoniously to her time out spot. Be as bland and uncommunicative as you can; no conversation, no lectures, just directly to time out.

- The time out spot should be away from the party. For me, the party is where the dog wants to be. If she wants to be at the door, her time out spot should be in a different room where she can't see, hear or relate to the party.

- A crate can be used for time out. That does not make the crate a bad thing. The discomfort for the dog is being removed from the party. How the dog relates to the crate will be determined by how the crate is normally used with the dog.

Our dogs are in crates at night and at other times when we or they need a break. Our dogs are always given treats when they're in their crates—except when they are in a time out. You can also use a safe room for time out. A safe room could be a laundry room, garage, basement or bathroom—any room where your dog has little entertainment and can't get into trouble.

- The dog remains in time out for a minimum of three to five minutes. The dog must be quiet and calm for the last three minutes she is in time out.

- If it takes the dog 20 minutes to calm down, the full time out would be 23 minutes. Don't worry, it doesn't usually take the dog long to learn that she does not get out unless she is quiet.

- Never go to a dog when she is making a fuss. It

teaches her that making a fuss will get her out of the time out. We want her to learn that being quiet gets her out of the time out.

- Obviously, don't put your dog in a crate if you think she will do damage to herself. If this is likely, you should be working with a certified trainer or behavior professional.

Remember my rules for good behavior: sitting, standing or lying down and not vocalizing. My dogs don't get out of the time out until they meet that standard. It's all about clarity with the dog. My dogs get ignored if they are making a fuss. My procedure for ignoring was explained in Section 19.

One of our dedicated clients rescued a Boxer. His wife told me that after beginning our training process, he actually waited two hours for the dog to settle down before he let her out of her crate. That's dedication. And that's what is sometimes necessary if a dog has been previously reinforced for an unwanted behavior. These unwanted behaviors are often unknowingly reinforced by owners who don't understand how the process works. When a dog is rescued, we often don't know the dog's background. In many cases, unbeknownst to their new owners, rescue dogs have been reinforced for undesirable behaviors.

- When the dog has been quiet for three minutes, I put her on a leash and take her out of the crate or safe room and back to the party. If the dog does the unwanted behavior again, I instantly mark it with "Too Bad" and again, unceremoniously take her back to time out (away from the party).

- Repeat this process as many times as you can stand it in a given setting. If you reach a point when you don't want to try again, leave the dog in the time out until the visitor is gone.

- The one thing you *do not* do is give in. You can repeat the process as many times as you can stand it, and you don't ever let the dog in to the party when she does the behavior you are working on.

- The dog needs to learn that every time she starts to lift her feet to start a jump, she hears your cue, "Too Bad," and she ends up out of the party.

- When the dog can enter the room and keep her feet on the ground, she gets to stay at the party.

- When jumping is the problem, you can help the dog be a winner by having her on a leash when a visitor comes to the house so you can immediately react to her behavior.

- When introducing the dog to a visitor, if it is safe, have the visitor offer a treat in an open hand at her side so the dog's focus is low and she is less likely to jump.

- You can also do this when your visitors have moved to your living area and are seated when you bring the dog in.

- Again, keep the dog on leash while she is learning. That way, you can immediately mark the undesired behavior and move the dog to time out. Don't use time out for more than one behavior at a time. It could confuse the dog. Clarity and simplicity are the keys here. The cue must be clear and immediately connected with the behavior in question. The move to time out is quick, without punishment or other interaction, just very matter-of-fact. Remember: clear, quick, simple—that's what makes it work.

Time out is just one strategy for your tool box. As you go through this book, you should be coming to understand that these principles, combined with your creativity and planning, offer many options for working with your dog.

Section 25:
More Complex Problems

Many client calls are for help with an "issue." These issues can be rooted in digging, barking, scratching, nipping, fighting, separation anxiety, severe anxiety or aggression. Those who call want us to know that except for the issues in question, their dog is great. They also want to know whether we have worked with problems like theirs before. And, they want to know if there is hope for a cure and how long it might take to fix it.

These callers have expectations that range from realistic to out of touch. Expectations can often sound like this: "All I want is for my dog to stay on my property; come every time I call; sit and lie down when I tell him; stay until I say he can leave; protect my house and family; and generally respect me as his master." All of these things are doable with the appropriate time commitment and expertise. I have found that few are doable in a six- to eight-week group class for around $90. Some issues are more annoying than dangerous, and can be resolved using simple management strategies.

If you find that you have an issue that persists after implementing my training protocol, check the Internet. There are organizations like the Dumb Friends League of Denver, Colorado, as well as websites maintained by private trainers, that have suggestions for dealing with specific behavior problems. When you are doing web research, you'll have to decide who to believe. You know the adage, "Just because you read it on the Internet, doesn't mean it's true," so check multiple sources and use common sense.

Hyper Dogs

"Can you settle my dog down? He won't listen; he's just hyper!" These are among the comments we hear the most at our training center. The reality is that during adolescence, many dogs seem to have a never-ending supply of energy. If that energy is not channeled, it can be really annoying. I often tell clients that adolescence is the most difficult time in the dog owner's life.

During this time, dogs test boundaries. This is the time when owners are looking for that benevolent farmer to provide acres of land so their dog can run free. If the owner does not have a management plan, many dogs are given away during adolescence. Some hope that spaying or neutering the dog will get rid of this extra energy. Sorry, this is not as good a solution as some have been led to believe. One estimate is that you have a 50-50 chance of seeing a difference in energy level after neutering a male dog, and probably very little difference after spaying a female.

The best approach to deal with this high energy is to develop a structure with definable, consistent boundaries. In addition, you must provide appropriate exercise, and put the effort into developing your training plan. If you do the things we suggest, your dog's hyperactivity and the annoying behaviors that go along with it can be managed.

As I explained earlier, rather than constantly trying to tell your dog not to do something, we suggest **teaching the dog what you <u>want</u> him to do**. "Settling" is a perfect example of a behavior that can be reinforced as conduct you actually *want*.

Mental Health Issues

As I mentioned earlier, trying to psychoanalyze a dog is fruitless, but there are some identifiable mental/emotional health issues that occur with dogs and often send folks looking for help.

To help you get a more personal feel for what these kinds of issues might be like for your dog, think about these examples.

- Are you a person who is generally okay about life, except that when you are in heavy traffic or when your in-laws come to visit, and you get anxious? This may be equivalent to a *mild case* of anxiety in a dog.

- Do you know someone who is very uncomfortable when he must balance his checkbook or go to a tax audit? That may be comparable to a *moderate case* of canine anxiety.

- How about the person who panics when they're even thinking about flying, or is incapacitated when speaking in public? Now you may be moving toward what it feels like for a dog who has *a severe anxiety issue*.

- Finally, what about the person who has so much rage that he or she becomes a spouse beater or bar fighter? Such a person can't be in certain situations without blowing up. Here you may be seeing extreme anxiety or lack of self-confidence—which parallels the root of *very serious aggression* in dogs.

Examples like these may help you better understand what it might be like for your dog if she has a problem that is based on anxiety. I think you are wise to consider what the dog may be *feeling*; not just be caught up in the worry, or fear of the *consequences* of the dog's actions.

Since we can't have a conversation with our dog to figure out what they are experiencing, the only feedback we get is what we observe about the dog and how he reacts when we attempt to help.

When we work with a dog on an issue that has a mental health component, our approach is based on available research, our personal experience and the experience of others who have dealt with similar issues.

Severe issues are always a challenge. There is no magic solution. Progress is about as easy to predict as it is for a person who is experiencing severe anxiety and is afraid to leave his home, or someone who thinks everyone is out to get her, or someone who has been mugged and insists on carrying a gun everywhere he goes. None of these problems are easily fixed.

For the human with these kinds of problems, his actions often seem perfectly logical to him. Likewise, for the dog, what we see as aberrant behavior makes perfect sense based on the dog's experience of a particular environment, situation, or the world in general.

For humans, we have counseling, support groups and (in many cases) medication to help a person reach a point where they can function in society. For owners, veterinarians, trainers and behavior professionals who want to help dogs with these kinds of issues, we have behavior modification and sometimes, medication. But we are no more able to predict a timetable or a specific result than we could do with a human. So again, consider what it might really be like for your dog, be realistic, don't ask for a miracle. If you get one, take it and be eternally thankful.

Separation Anxiety

Separation anxiety is a common example of a canine mental health issue. This condition can be mild or it can be so severe that a dog may actually damage herself if left alone. Typically, a dog with separation anxiety will have an anxiety response within about 30 minutes after being left alone by her owner.

Behaviors associated with separation anxiety include digging, chewing and scratching at doors or windows - seemingly in an attempt to escape. Howling, barking and crying are also common, possibly to call the owner home. Urination and defecation can occur, even with dogs that are housetrained. All of these behaviors can occur at an extreme level and can result not only in damage to the dog, but also to the house. Floors may be torn up, walls broken through, curtains pulled down, and furniture destroyed.

All of this has happened to our clients. All of this happens as the dog moves into a panic state as a result of the stress of being left alone. None of these things are done because the dog has been trying to "get even" or is "mad" because the owner has left her alone. It is strictly a result of severe anxiety tied to a panic response.

A dog may experience separation anxiety under these circumstances:

- When a dog who is expecting constant human companionship is left alone.

- When a dog is left alone after being on vacation with the family.

- When a dog is taken on vacation and left in a strange environment.

I actually had a client who reported the cost of their vacation was increased by $1500 when they had to pay for repairs to a bedroom in a rented house. They took their newly adopted dog on vacation with them and shortly after checking in, locked the dog in a bedroom and went to dinner.

They came back to find a disaster. In fairness, and in retrospect, they realized that the dog had no way of seeing this as an exciting opportunity to be with them, all he knew is that he was in a totally strange place and everyone he knew and loved just left him there. He panicked. We also have no idea what may have been occurring at the doors or windows that might have added to his angst.

- After the dog has spent time in a shelter or a boarding kennel.

- When there is a change in the family's routine or work schedule.

- When the family moves to a new home.

- In association with the addition of, or loss of, a family member.

Because behaviors associated with separation anxiety can also occur for other reasons, it's important to verify that these behaviors are occurring when the dog is left alone. Dogs with separation anxiety tend to follow their owner from room to room, display frantic greetings and act excitedly when the owner prepares to leave.

If you suspect your dog has separation anxiety, call your dog's veterinarian, trainer or behavior professional to help you assess the situation and develop a plan to help the dog. Frequently, that plan involves the use of medication along with a carefully designed behavior modification program.

Some people make the mistake of trying to cure the situation using medication only. The best results involve the use of both medication and behavior modification. Medication by itself doesn't teach the dog how to cope or what to expect in a situation, but it can be very beneficial in achieving results when used in conjunction with a behavior plan as developed with your qualified trainer/behavior consultant.

Because you are dealing with a panic response, punishment is not usually an effective way to deal with separation anxiety.

Aggression

In some cases, a dog's response to confusion or mixed messages from their owners may be seen as aggression. This "aggression" often proves scary to the humans involved. In many cases, an owner's response to this "aggression" is to confront or punish the dog. If the dog then reacts to the owner's punishment, the next move may be to remove the dog from the home.

Some people think the best way to deal with this kind of problem is by having a trainer or a behavior professional have a "talk" with their dog—meaning "teach the dog a lesson" (involving punishment in some form). In our experience, that does not translate into an improvement in the dog's behavior back home.

Each person with a perceived dog aggression problem also has an idea about what they hope the solution will be. When it's two dogs attacking each other, the desired solution may be that the two dogs get along again without supervision. Fortunately, many aggression-related issues can be resolved. Unfortunately, some cannot be worked out in the way a client might imagine.

Some problems may only be resolved by the use of good management techniques. For people who live a busy life, work two jobs or have little children, *management* may not be desirable or realistic. For clients with these, or similar lifestyle realities, serious soul searching is required. I'd rather see a dog be re-homed, than take a chance on the safety of children or the elderly/infirm, in a home where management is not realistic.

Discussing the situation with a professional may help you better sort things out, and experience less guilt, if the decision is to remove the dog from the home.

Owner Fear

As I mentioned earlier, if you are afraid of your dog, your situation becomes more complex. Denying that you are afraid of your dog is even worse. Fear makes us do things we wouldn't otherwise do. So my word to you is, "If something your dog has done or is doing scares you, get help immediately!" Discuss your concerns with a behavior professional or your veterinarian.

You always have options. The longer you let a difficult situation go unaddressed, the fewer options you may have.

If your dog is acting in an aggressive manner, get help immediately. Once a dog bites and causes damage, most rescue organizations are hesitant to help.

It is vitally important that you disclose any bite history or signs of aggression when you talk with a veterinarian or behavior worker. Not doing so could come back to haunt you.

Again, if you have children or the elderly/infirm living with you and if your dog might bite, is large, or could cause serious damage, you may need to consider re-homing.

Section 26:
Supplements and Medications

Since I'm not a veterinarian, even writing generally about supplements and medication, leaves me open to criticism. Suffice it to say this topic will be considered in layman's terms. Your veterinarian should be your expert resource when dealing with supplements and medication. My purpose is to give a general overview of how supplements and medications may be used in conjunction with training and behavior work.

Definition of Supplements

The term "supplement" can be used for anything from vitamins to calming tablets. Various powders, oils, pills and aromas are used to provide support for dogs. Brand names such as Rescue Remedy, Comfort Zone and DAP are examples of products that have been around long enough to be recognizable. There are many more.

Dogs who have anxiety that may be contributing to behavior problems can often be helped with appropriate use of a supplement or medication. I often describe the options this way: A supplement or medication may be used to help take the edge off of the dog's anxiety. If a veterinarian has made the referral to us, he or she may already have prescribed a medication program to be used along with our behavior plan.

DAP Collar

If not, and if I sense that a supplement or medication might help the dog, I suggest that the client may want to consider using a DAP (dog-appeasing hormone) collar. A DAP collar looks like a flea collar but has an inert block attached that has a hormone imbedded. DAP is a manufactured hormone that creates an "all is well with the world" feeling in some dogs. The heat of the dog's body releases the hormone.

I see the DAP collar as an entry-level attempt to ease the dog's anxiety. We have had positive results with this device. DAP also comes in spray, atomizer and wipes. I like the collar because it is always with the dog. The collar lasts about 30 days. The spray can also be used on a bandana around the dog's neck and applied to bedding.

Rescue Remedy

Another old stand-by for dog owners is Rescue Remedy, a homeopathic mixture that is given to the dog in water or directly by mouth. It is administered in minute amounts. It is intended to calm the dog. Likewise, scents such as lavender are sometimes used to help relax the dog. There are those in the healing community who specialize in these kinds of supportive supplements. There are nutritionists, herbalists and holistic veterinarians to advise you about the use of this growing list of supplements and other alternative remedies.

Prescriptions

Veterinarians may prescribe tranquilizers or anti-anxiety drugs if deemed appropriate. Tranquilizers are sometimes used for short-term support. Anti-anxiety drugs may be used more long-term. Within these options, there are brands of medication that have been specifically formulated for and tested on dogs and there are those that are manufactured for humans. In some situations, veterinarians may prescribe for your dog a drug made for humans.

If your dog is put on tranquilizers, you may notice the effects. The dog may even seem a little tired or sluggish. If he's on anti-anxiety medications, you may not notice anything overt other than the fact that your dog may be a little less edgy. Tranquilizers may take effect very quickly, while anti-anxiety medications such as fluoxetine (Prozac) and clomipramine (Clomicalm) may take a few weeks to make a difference.

Side Effects

With any drug, there is a potential for side effects. Determining the appropriate dosage may take time and may require several contacts with your veterinarian. You may be asked to give updates on your dog so the veterinarian can adjust the dosage of the medication. In some situations, it may take some trial and error for the veterinarian to find the right medication and the correct dosage for your dog. Occasionally, it is not possible to find a helpful medication.

A Beneficial Mix

Current thinking supports use of medication in combination with training and behavior work. The drug alone doesn't teach the dog anything, so using training in conjunction with the medication has the potential for you to reap the greatest benefit. For some owners, the idea of their dog being put on drugs is uncomfortable. My perspective is to look at it from the dog's standpoint. It is the dog, not the owner, who has the anxiety and in fact may be suffering every day as a result. When an owner arbitrarily rules out the use of medication, it is usually done without consideration of what it may mean for the dog.

Section 27:
Problem Solving Strategy

Once your basics are in place, you are in a position to tackle specific problems that you and your companion may be experiencing. If you have never developed a plan to address a specific behavior change, following are the mechanics of how it is done. What I have found to be the most powerful element in this process (intuition) will be explored in the next section.

Behaviors vs. Labels

The first step is to move past mere labels ("Rover barks all the time") to specific accurate behavior descriptions that have clarified the situation more precisely (*"Rover barks for 10 minutes whenever I tie him to the tree behind the house in the afternoon"*). A mere label can't be quantified or specifically addressed, whereas a behavior description can be. Some more examples:

"My dog tears my house apart" - *When I go to work, my dog is loose in the apartment. When I get home, the waste basket is turned over, and its contents strewn across the floor.*

"My dog is aggressive" – *When I let a stranger in my front door, my dog stands beside me and barks and shows his teeth.*

"My dog is a jumper" – *When I get home from work, my dog jumps up on me and licks my face.*

As you think about the problem behaviors you are experiencing, don't be distressed if several come to mind. This is not unusual. Just take time to define the actual behaviors (what happens, when, where, and with whom). Check with other family members to be sure the list is complete and the behavior observations are also what they all experience, noting if there are any clear differences in what they observe.

Prioritize

With your home training team, decide on the top issue you all agree needs to be addressed first. At this starting point, and throughout this process, you want the **consensus and support of your team**. Be cautious about moving too quickly in your vote or final decision. You don't want to run roughshod over any team member or create winners and losers in the decision process, because to do so only causes resentment and undermines your team's success.

Brainstorm

Use brainstorming to identify possible ways to reach your desired behavior change. Remember that even though it may appear that there is only one path available, **there is always more than one option.**

Good brainstorming aims at **generating a large number of ideas,** and doesn't criticize or limit the flow of possibilities. Let everyone contribute ideas. This large ingathering of options is what you want. You can also include Internet research, rereading parts of this book, and asking for ideas from other dog owners with well-mannered pets.

Don't rush to decide on your course. Initial brainstorming actually primes the pump of your thinking process, and you are wise to let your subconscious mind have some time to percolate (continue mulling the ideas).

Once all team members have contributed, and had time to contemplate the ideas that you all generated, you can begin culling them down to the best solution that meets your criteria:

- It aims directly at our desired goal

- It is practical for our situation

- It doesn't appear that it will generate any new or bigger problems.

- It fits with our values, including being fair to the dog.

- Having taken time to consider the options, we all agree it is the best choice.

Detailed Plan

Now you undertake the critical process of devising a carefully thought-out implementation plan. This is where you focus on the actual *who, what, where, when, and how* of the solution. When all concur that they understand the plan, and what their own part in it will be, it is helpful to write it out (it doesn't need to be fancy) and post it where all can see it.

As you work your plan, remember that you're staying focused and flexible – keep assessing if the plan is moving in the direction you want and make course corrections if needed. Any glitch that emerges is nothing more than a new or unforeseen problem that needs to be analyzed and solved. If needed, seek out the help of a trainer or behavior specialist.

I'll be honest with you. When working with a dog who has complex behavior problems, or who is in a complex environment, a path to resolution isn't always clear. In these situations, I can find myself engaged with, and sometimes consumed by, the problem all my waking hours. My waking hours can even be lengthened because the problem is so much on my mind that sleep doesn't come easily. During such times, I am very much aware that my *intuition* is at work.

Section 28:
Intuition

As I mentioned in the last section, I highly value intuition as a tool. No matter how concrete we may believe we are in using fact-based rational processes in our problem-solving, when all is said and done, something within us says, "This is what makes sense. This is what adds up." This is **intuition**, and it's at its strongest when hard science is scant, incomplete or inconclusive.

To help you develop a satisfying relationship with your pet, I believe intuition can be very valuable. Here is what I've found that helps cultivate your developing intuition.

Something to think about: *Thomas Edison was once asked where he got his ideas. His answer was that, "they are floating around in the air." Nikola Tesla said he got many of his best ideas while daydreaming. Einstein said he grasped his theory of relativity while "daydreaming."*

Definition of Intuition

Dictionary definitions for intuition say things like: Knowledge obtained without rational thought; innate or instinctive knowledge; immediate comprehension, or cognition; "knowing that you know"; a hunch or a gut feeling; and a realization that may arrive in a seemingly magical moment, possibly after a long pondering of the problem.

I often find that a solution appears after a period of pondering the problem. **I call it an Ignition Point.** It's when all the raw material I've gathered up, and have been mulling over, bursts into a robust fire and I can see my way forward on an issue. There is a bit of magic to it, because you don't know when that instantaneous combustion will happen, or what it will yield.

Clarifying the Problem

Knowing I have a perplexing problem to solve, I state it clearly to myself - "I need to find a way to train Rover not to bark when I release him in our fenced yard."

I gather fuel for my intuition by the raw material I think about (observations, facts, brainstormed ideas, etc.). I stay open to being ignited in unexpected ways, but I don't force the process.

Where Intuition Takes Place

Intuition can kick in amidst our conscious thoughts, but it also functions in the background at times that are totally separated from current issues.

Those times can include when you sleep, eat lunch or drive, as well as while being stimulated in other ways, such as off-topic conversations, watching a movie, listening to music, attending inspiring lectures, or exercising. They tend to come as little bursts of "knowing" that we need to practice capturing – either by writing them down, or making a quick note in a smart phone. They could be thought fragments, streams of thought, or even entire solutions.

Gathering these "bits" and thinking about them later will enable us to see if they coalesce into a whole, or are not useful at all. Occasionally, these **"knowings"** are shot down when talking with others about the problem. Even those flashes that don't prove to be "the answer" can still serve as a conduit that leads to a better decision.

Enhancing Intuition

For the purpose of improving your relationship with your dog, let me offer these ideas to enhance your intuition.

Be fearless about gathering your raw material. Don't fret that your thoughts are not yet clear – trust that your subconscious mind is at work for you.

Make time for intentional daydreaming. Preferably, this is done in a quiet setting where people are not likely to disturb you. Some people lean back in their comfortable chair. Others add soft music. Still others go to a favorite outdoor spot. Some like to hear birds singing, wind blowing, water rippling, or waves crashing on a beach.

The secret is not to have an agenda. Allow your mind to drift and contemplate with no expectations about results or how and when they may show up. For some, awareness will occur during this time of reflection; for others it may show up at a later time, often when least expected.

Prayer is another way to enhance intuition. With your intention clearly in mind, and according to your religious affiliation or spiritual beliefs, enter into a prayerful state and ask in the appropriate way for guidance that will allow you to best reach a solution. Again, answers may not be immediate.

Don't Force It

Trust that your intuition and creativity are at work. Don't set up expectations about what, how, or when things should happen. No matter which approach you decide to use, follow your own path. Making time for intuition is not another "to do" list item, but rather, it is intentionally putting the list aside, and cultivating purposeful "downtime."

Pay attention to your environment and notice where you tend to get the best results. Is it when you are sitting, lying down, at the park, in the woods, on the lake, while jogging? I have had good results from just giving it another day if I run into a frustrating situation. I'm often amazed at how things clear up a day later.

What You May Experience

Results may be subtle to dramatic. Obviously, if the result of your chosen course provides you with a startling revelation, the process will seem valid.

You may be startled by a very concrete thought that says, "do this" (sometimes really big, sometimes not). This could include an unexplained feeling that you need to talk to a particular person or to browse a particular bookshelf. You might even find yourself with an urge to attend a particular seminar, where - lo and behold - a speaker, maybe one you were not planning to hear, says something that provides just what you need.

If you do not experience a "Eureka" moment, take heart – the process is simply not over. In some cases, it may take a form or present a message that you are not yet ready to acknowledge. It's not that your intuition has abandoned you. The more you use your intuition, the easier it may be for you to recognize its messages, even under pressure.

A helpful thing to aid your intuition is to identify problems or situations *early*, so that your intuition can work with less pressure, over time. A last-minute crisis, dealt with under high stress, may not be the best time to say, "Intuition, don't fail me now!"

When you have a prompting to seek out someone else's wisdom, ask them open-ended questions and really *listen* to their suggestions. Resist the temptation to cut them off or counter their views (remember, you sought *them* out because they know their stuff.) Take notes and ask questions to clarify anything you did not understand. This new input may help you reach an ignition point.

You may also find that you get an idea to try something that isn't a fully formed plan, but rather a step toward it. I would encourage you to try it and then continue to allow your thinking and intuition to work using the results of that idea.

If you work with others, always run ideas by your team, and if you discover that your ideas are out of sync with those you are working with, both dog and human, stay open to making needed changes.

In the end, only you know what you are comfortable using with your companion. Combining the facts that you have with your *intuition*, your *gut sense, can* lead you, but, as I've said numerous times, "If anything I've suggested in this book, or which you want to try with your dog, seems risky or dangerous, get the help of a professional trainer"

Section 29: Final Words

Remember My Goal

In ending this book, I would like to be sure one thing is clear. **This book is intended to help build a foundation for a great relationship between humans and dogs.** If that foundation is built early, many problems will be prevented. If problems already exist, this model becomes the basis upon which we begin problem-solving. The foundation we outlined herein becomes the structure within which additional planning takes place.

A Consistent Teaching Approach

When explaining our approach, I have been meticulous in laying out how we teach. As a dog owner, you need to be so consistent in the way you teach your dog, that **he can tell when you are trying to start something new because he recognizes your approach.**

Nothing Takes Place in a Vacuum

Frequently, I am called upon to explain that a dog's behavior does not occur in a vacuum; it occurs within whatever structure exists in the dog's life. As I explained in Section 12 on Groundwork, accurately assessing the situation in which the dog lives, and how his owners are relating to him, has to precede implementing my protocol.

What I have included in this book is my adaptation of the great deal of information I have digested over the decades, and integrated into my own approach. Listing authors and professionals who I have gleaned from in that time would add 40 pages of references, and would have to include the ones who gave me great ideas, *as well as* those from whom I learned what *not* to do.

I offer a sincere "thank you" to all who contributed to my growth and helped build the body of knowledge that now exists. This book is intended to be one more helpful tool in that collection.

About the Author

Jim and his wife, Dr. Charlene Akenhead, have bred and trained Shepherds and Malamutes for 50 years. In 1995, Jim and his son Matt, formed Signature K-9 Training and Behavior LLC in northeastern Ohio. Signature K-9 did about two-thirds of its work in private consultations. About half their work was with difficult dogs, including classes for reactive and shy dogs. Now Jim and Charlene reside in southern Virginia, where they continue to help dogs become family members.

Jim has five earned degrees, including a Doctorate in Research and Education as well as a Masters Degree in Counseling. He is certified as a canine trainer and behavior consultant by four independent organizations. He is listed in seven *Who's Who* anthologies on leadership and has been recognized as a Distinguished Alumni by Bowling Green State University (Ohio). Along with his wife, Charlene, Jim was chosen as Business and Professional Person of the Year in their community.

Jim has presented at local and national conferences, has taught in the Canine Behavior Program at Kutztown University, and founded a Canine Behavior Program at Youngstown State University, Ohio. He frequently presents his views on canine aggression.

Jim is the author of four other books. He is a member of the International Association of Animal Behavior Consultants and the Certification Council for Professional Dog Trainers, and has served two terms on the board of directors of each.

He was director of National K-9 Trainers Association, an organization with members in 50 states and 30 countries. He is also a professional member of the Association of Professional Dog Trainers, APDT, the International Association of Canine Professionals, IACP, and he helped start two local therapy dog groups.

If you have a question about dog behavior or training, check our website:

www.signaturek9dogtraining.com

---

www.ingramcontent.com/pod-product-compliance
Lightning Source LLC
Chambersburg PA
CBHW020353170426
43200CB00005B/158